D0849814

Celebrities with Heart

Hilary Duff

Celebrity with Heart

Laura B. Edge

Enslow Publishers, Inc.
40 Industrial Road
Box 398
Berkeley Heights, NJ 07922
USA

http://www.enslow.com

Library of Congress Cataloging-in-Publication Data

Edge, Laura Bufano, 1953–
    Hilary Duff : celebrity with heart / Laura B. Edge.
        p. cm. — (Celebrities with heart)
    Summary: "A biography of American actress and singer Hilary Duff"—
        Provided by publisher.
    Includes bibliographical references and index.
    ISBN-13: 978-0-7660-3404-4
    1. Duff, Hilary, 1987—Juvenile literature. 2. Actors—United States—Biography—
        Juvenile literature. 3. Singers—United States—Biography—Juvenile literature.
        I. Title.
    PN2287.D79E34 2010
    792.02'8'092—dc22
    [B]
                                                            2009023810

ISBN-13: 978-1-59845-205-1 (paperback)

Printed in the United States of America

052010 Lake Book Manufacturing, Inc., Melrose Park, IL

10 9 8 7 6 5 4 3 2 1

To Our Readers: We have done our best to make sure all Internet Addresses in this book were
active and appropriate when we went to press. However, the author and the publisher have
no control over and assume no liability for the material available on those Internet sites or
on other Web sites they may link to. Any comments or suggestions can be sent by e-mail to
comments@enslow.com or to the address on the back cover.

Every effort has been made to locate all copyright holders of material used in this book. If
any errors or omissions have occurred, corrections will be made in future editions of
this book.

♻ Enslow Publishers, Inc., is committed to printing our books on recycled paper. The paper
in every book contains 10% to 30% post-consumer waste (PCW). The cover board on the
outside of each book contains 100% PCW. Our goal is to do our part to help young people
and the environment too!

Contents

Hilary Duff

Giving Back

On May 22, 2008, twenty-year-old Hilary Duff visited Boca Raton Elementary School in Boca Raton, Florida. The students had decorated the walls of the cafeteria with "We Love You, Hilary" posters. They cheered when she arrived wearing a sunny yellow blouse and blue-jean shorts. Duff is an actress, but she was not filming a movie. She is a singer, but she was not there to sing. She had come to make sure the students had enough food to eat.

Hilary Duff is passionate about feeding America's hungry children. According to a survey by the Department of Agriculture, more than 12 million children and teens in the United States suffer from hunger. "I understand that children in other countries are starving and hungry," said Duff, "but what many Americans don't understand is that there is an alarming amount of people right here in America who go to bed hungry and wake up hungry because they don't have the resources to buy food."[1]

Teachers at Boca Raton Elementary had noticed that some of their students had a hard time paying attention on Mondays. They discovered that 64 percent of the school's students were hungry on weekends. This affected their ability to focus on their schoolwork. "We're expecting kids to show up to school on Monday and learn and grow with no fuel in their body," said Duff.[2]

Hilary Duff traveled to Florida to help launch Blessings in a Backpack at Boca Raton Elementary. She learned about the program when she heard her mother, Susan Duff, and Blessings in a Backpack founder, Stan Curtis, talking about the number of hungry children in America. On school days, most of them participate in school lunch programs. But on weekends, many do not have enough food to eat. "I was shocked," said Duff, "and ready to do whatever I could to get involved and help to fix this problem."[3]

Stan Curtis started Blessings in a Backpack in 2005. The program was designed to make sure children get enough food to eat on weekends. Each week, volunteers stuff backpacks with healthy food. Students take the backpacks home on Fridays to enjoy the food over the weekend.

Boca Raton community leaders joined Hilary Duff in bringing the program to Boca Raton Elementary School. City council member Susan Haynie declared the day Blessings in a Backpack Day. The students came up with their own name for the special day. They called it Hilary Duff Day.

Duff spoke at an assembly for students who participate in the program. She listened to the student choir, posed for pictures, gave hugs, and chatted with the children. "I love to give back and when I see people smile, no money can pay that amount," she said.[4] The students presented Hilary Duff with handmade cards and a bouquet of flowers.

After the assembly, Duff joined the volunteers at Boca Raton Community Church to stuff backpacks for the students she had met. They filled the backpacks with healthy food such as fruit cups, bread, peanut butter, milk, juice, and canned beef stew. Students took the backpacks home and were able to have enough food to eat over the weekend. They brought the empty backpacks back to school on Monday to be filled for the next weekend.

Duff financially sponsors Blessings in a Backpack at a school in Los Angeles, California. "This is a program that really works," she said, "and it's completely pure. When I give my check to my school each month, 100 percent, every last cent goes toward food. Nobody gets paid, you don't have to buy backpacks, we find a way to get it all donated."[5]

As spokesperson for Blessings in a Backpack, Hilary Duff works to increase awareness of child hunger. She speaks at fund-raisers and convinces people to get involved, make a donation, or sponsor a school. She also travels around the country to bring Blessings in a Backpack into schools. She has visited schools in Indiana, New York City, and Kentucky. Duff enjoys meeting the children and seeing the impact of the program. "You come to the school and it makes it all real, you get to see the people that are taking the food home this weekend and are getting to feed their brothers and sisters at home," she said.[6]

The students appreciate her visits. After Duff helped launch Blessings in a Backpack at a school in Indiana, ten-year-old Juwan Long said, "It was good because she touched my hand and I'm never washing it again."[7]

Teachers immediately saw positive results from the program. Children were alert and ready to work on Mondays. Test scores went up because they could

Hilary Duff hands backpacks full of food to students at a New York City elementary school in 2008 during a Blessings in a Backpack event.

concentrate on learning instead of their hunger. In 2009, the program was feeding children in thirty-seven schools. Duff and Curtis hope to expand that number to more than sixty.

Hilary Duff also works with America's largest all-volunteer food distribution group, USA Harvest. This group, also started by Stan Curtis, is dedicated to wiping out hunger in the United States. The mission is to move food from people who have too much to those who have too little. Volunteers pick up surplus food from restaurants, hospitals, and food suppliers and deliver it to missions, soup kitchens, and people in need. Duff has donated millions of meals through USA Harvest. She often serves food at homeless shelters. She also hosts "Food for a Friend" drives at her concerts. She encourages fans to bring canned food to the concerts. The food is then distributed to homeless shelters in the town where the concert takes place.

Duff uses a blog on her Web site to keep her fans informed of her activities and travel schedule. She often thanks them for their support and for helping to provide food for hungry Americans. After one of her concert tours, she wrote, "Everyone supported our food drive with USA Harvest and raised about 432 thousand pounds of food, which adds up to over 800 thousand meals which will feed people who are hungry right here in our own country! It is important to understand that if we work together, we can make a difference in peoples lives. . . . I hope u guys know how special each and every one of you is to me!"[8]

Kids With a Cause (KWAC) is another one of Hilary Duff's favorite charities. She began working with the group in 1999, when she was a young girl in Hollywood hoping to launch an acting career. KWAC encourages children to help children. It teaches the principles and practices of philanthropy to children and teens in the entertainment business. Young entertainers spend time with children who are facing difficult challenges. They provide a helping hand to "children who, through no fault of their own, suffer from poverty, illness or lack of education."[9] They also help children who have been abandoned, neglected, or abused.

Duff visits children in hospitals, group homes, orphanages, and homeless shelters. She hangs out with sick children and tries to lift their spirits. Sometimes she colors or paints with them. Sometimes she sings or dances. But mostly, she chats with young people and takes their minds off their pain and discouragement. Duff also promotes the KWAC literacy program. She often reads to students who come from low-income families and may not have books of their own.

Hilary Duff encourages teens to get involved in their communities and find ways to help people who are less fortunate. She tells young people to organize a food drive, visit sick children, or help clean up the environment. Duff spends a lot of time and energy helping others. She reminds her fans that "giving is something that is easy to do."[10]

Hilary Duff greets a young cancer patient during an event in Washington, D.C., in 2005. Giving back to the community, especially children in need, is important to Duff, and she encourages her fans to help.

Animal-lover Hilary

Hilary Duff works with charities that help animals. She and her sister, Haylie, encourage people to adopt pets at their local shelters. "We love to take animals that don't have a home and put them with people who we know need the love but who will care for and take care of their pet like a family member."[11]

Hilary Duff celebrated her twenty-first birthday on September 28, 2008. Fans from the United States, Canada, Mexico, England, Italy, the Netherlands, and Australia created a video birthday card for her. They sent good wishes for her birthday and thanked her for all she does to help others. Stephanie, a fan club member from Malta, wrote, "Hilary I hope you have a lovely day that holds one bright moment after another! You are the most generous, caring and kindest person I have ever seen, and you deserve the most wonderful birthday ever!"[12]

Fans also thanked Duff for being someone they could look up to. Her fan club wrote this verse:

> *Hilary, God gave a gift to the world when you were born—*
> *a person who loves, who cares,*
> *who sees a person's need and fills it,*
> *. . . someone who touches each life she enters,*
> *and makes a difference in the world.*[13]

Helping others is natural for Hilary Duff. She began early, when she was a young girl in Texas.

The Early Years

Hilary Duff was born on September 28, 1987, in Houston, Texas. Her father, Bob Duff, owned and managed a chain of convenience stores. Her mother, Susan Duff, sold cosmetics and worked as a home-maker. Two-and-a-half-year-old Haylie welcomed her baby sister home. The family lived in Houston for a few years, then moved to the small town of Boerne, about thirty miles northwest of San Antonio in the Texas hill country.

The Duff family also owned a ranch near Bastrop, thirty-three miles southeast of Austin. Hilary spent lots of time playing outside, under the wide-open Texas sky.

She jumped rope, played tag and hide-and-seek, and jumped on her backyard trampoline. She liked to swim, climb trees, and turn cartwheels.

From an early age, Hilary demonstrated a flair for the dramatic. She had her own sense of style and definite ideas about fashion. When she was three, she begged her mother to let her wear red glitter shoes every day. "They went with everything—in her mind," said her mother.[1]

Hilary was a born animal lover. She and her family often went to fairs, livestock shows, and rodeos. When she was around four years old, she wanted to be a veterinarian. She changed her mind when she found out that veterinarians sometimes have to put sick animals to sleep. Hilary rescued two dogs from an animal shelter: Little Dog, a fox terrier/Chihuahua mix and Remington, a border collie. They became her beloved pets. "I think having a special animal in your life can help anyone learn to appreciate nature more," she said. "And a horse can become your best friend, just like a dog. Both have a strong sense of loyalty."[2]

Hilary and Haylie had Shetland ponies to ride on the ranch near Austin. Hilary loved being around ponies and horses. "Our favorites were the brown and white brother and sister Shetlands that we named Cinnamon and Sugar," she said. "They were really beautiful and quite small—the perfect size for us. Cinnamon was mine.

She had a bit of a diva attitude with others, but she was really very sweet with me."[3]

Hilary learned early in life to help others and do her best to make the world a better place. When her parents threw Christmas parties, they asked the guests to bring charitable donations rather than gifts. Hilary and her mom collected food from friends and family to donate to local food banks. When Hilary rode bikes with her dad, they often stopped to pick up trash in the neighborhood as part of the excursion. "Our parents taught us it's the little things you can do that can make such a big improvement in our lives as well as the lives of others," said Hilary.[4]

The Duff sisters enjoyed playing dress-up. Hilary and Haylie liked to wear the most outrageous costumes they could find and perform skits. They sang and danced for each other, their parents, their neighbors, and anyone else who would listen. The girls watched television shows and then turned off the set and acted out the scenes they had seen. Big sister Haylie assigned the parts. Since she had long hair, Haylie played the girl's roles. She made Hilary play the boy's parts because Hilary had short hair.

Like many younger sisters, Hilary adored her big sister. She tried to be just like Haylie. Haylie took ballet lessons. She liked to come home and show Hilary what she had learned. Before long, Hilary took ballet lessons too. She enjoyed the classes and thought about becoming a professional dancer. When she was six years old, Hilary made her stage debut. She and Haylie performed in a touring company production of the Christmas ballet *The Nutcracker.*

Hilary attended first and second grades at St. Mary's Hall, a private school in San Antonio. St. Mary's, founded in 1879, was known for its performing arts program. Haylie took acting classes at an acting workshop near their home. She performed in school plays and dreamed of becoming an actress. Susan Duff asked Hilary if she wanted to take acting classes too, but Hilary was not interested in acting. "I thought it was so stupid," she said, "and I would never want to do that."[5]

Hilary changed her mind when she saw all the neat things Haylie had learned. She wanted to do everything her sister did. So, before long, Hilary was taking acting classes too. "I just kind of followed in Haylie's footsteps," she said.[6]

The girls soon had their mother driving them to auditions all over Texas. They auditioned for local theater productions and television commercials. Hilary's first television appearance was for a Texas cable company commercial. Haylie also landed a few commercials and both girls did some modeling. Their success convinced Susan Duff to take the girls to Los Angeles, California,

Haylie (left) and Hilary Duff attend a benefit for St. Jude Children's Research Hospital in 2008. Hilary Duff's fans have big sister Haylie to thank for inspiring Hilary to act. Hilary had no interest in acting until she saw her sister doing it and thought it would be fun to take acting classes too.

Television Pilots

A television pilot is a single, first episode of a television show. Every year TV network executives view hundreds of pilots and decide which shows they think audiences will like. When they think a show will draw a large audience, they order more episodes to be filmed and add the show to the television schedule.

to audition. Hilary and Haylie both appeared in commercials in L.A. Hilary thought, "This is so easy!"[7]

The Duffs returned to Texas, but Hilary was hooked on acting. In 1996, when she was nine, she attended an acting seminar in San Antonio. Hilary met a talent agent there who suggested the family move to Los Angeles. In L.A., the capital of the entertainment industry, Hilary and her sister could take acting classes and audition for the television pilot season. The pilot season is the few months when television producers cast actors for television shows. It is an important time for fledgling actors.

Hilary and Haylie talked their parents into moving to California so they could audition for more roles. They found a manager in Texas who offered to set up lots of auditions in Los Angeles for them in exchange for one thousand dollars. Susan Duff paid her the fee and rented an apartment in Hollywood for six months for herself and the girls. Bob Duff stayed in Houston to manage his business. He flew to Los Angeles every three weeks to visit.

The manager turned out to be a fraud. The Duffs settled into their temporary home, but they never saw or heard from her again. They realized they had a lot to learn about the entertainment industry. Susan Duff sprang into action. She supported her daughters' dreams and did all she could to help them achieve their goals. She bought a shelfful of books about the entertainment business, studied them, and learned about the unique world of Hollywood. She acted as her daughters' manager. She sent packets of information about the girls to agents and casting directors. She made countless telephone calls to set up auditions and listened to agents hang up on her time and time again. "My mother has been the number-one person to help us do what we want to do," said Hilary.[8]

Susan Duff's hard work paid off. In 1997, Hilary and Haylie both earned small roles in the television miniseries

True Women. Their roles in the romantic Western were so small that they did not get screen credit for their parts. But they got the opportunity to work with well-known actors, including Angelina Jolie and Dana Delany. The thrill of being in a miniseries fueled their desire to act.

Before long Hilary and Haylie were able to hire an experienced manager. They went to every audition that called for girls their age. But there were thousands of hopeful children trying out for the same roles. Competition was fierce and they faced a lot of rejection. Sometimes the sisters tried out for the same role. Their parents worried that they would become jealous of each other if one sister got a part and the other did not. They talked to both girls about the importance of supporting each other, of being a family. Hilary's father felt so strongly about the girls remaining close that he threatened to bring them back to Texas if they ever fought over roles.

Hilary learned to overcome discouragement. For two years, she went to one audition after another and did not get any roles. But she knew she wanted to act, so she kept going. Her mom encouraged her to follow her dreams. "My mom is very optimistic about things," she said.[9] When Hilary auditioned for a role and did not get the part, Susan Duff reminded her to keep a positive attitude. "So what?" she told her daughter. "You have an audition tomorrow and the next day, so what are you even worried about?"[10] Susan Duff also let Hilary know that if she wanted to stop auditioning and go back to Texas, that was fine too. Her mother's attitude gave Hilary strength and comfort through the many no's she faced along the way.

In 1998, Haylie landed the role of Gina Adams, a cousin of the Addams family, in the film *The Addams Family Reunion*. A month later, Hilary won the lead role in the direct-to-video movie *Casper Meets Wendy*. She acted opposite the animated Casper the Friendly Ghost. Hilary played the good witch Wendy. In the film, Casper and Wendy become great friends. They team up to defeat an evil warlock. In the process, they learn to appreciate and accept the fact that they are different from the other members of their families.

Hilary had fun making the film, and she learned a lot about how movies are made. She also had some embarrassing moments on the set. In one scene, she was supposed to run around and chase a goat. The director yelled, "Meaner! Meaner!" So, Hilary ran faster with an angry expression on her face. The director yelled, "Cut!" and asked Hilary what she was doing. She told the director she was following his instructions and acting mean. The director explained that he was not talking to

Hilary and her ghostly costar Casper from the 1998 film *Casper Meets Wendy.* This was Hilary's first starring role in a movie.

her when he gave those orders. He was calling the goat, whose name was Meaner.

The Young Artist Awards committee nominated Hilary for Best Leading Young Actress Age Ten or Under for her role as Wendy. Although she did not win the award, she was thrilled by the nomination. It boosted her confidence as an actress.

After *Casper Meets Wendy*, Hilary continued to audition for roles in movies and television. In 1999, she was cast in the supporting role of Ellie in the TV movie *The Soul Collector*. The movie was filmed in Texas, so Hilary was able to spend time at home while she made the film. She worked with Melissa Gilbert, former child star of the hit television series *Little House on the Prairie*. The story centered on an angel sent to live among humans for a month. Hilary's performance earned rave reviews. She won the Young Artists Award for Best Performance in a TV Movie or Pilot—Supporting Young Actress.

In 2000, Hilary appeared in an episode of the medical TV drama *Chicago Hope*. In this dramatic role, she

School Must Go On

Even though she spent a lot of her time auditioning, Hilary still had to keep up with her studies. For a while, Susan Duff home-schooled Hilary. When she was filming a movie, a teacher tutored Hilary on the set. Her favorite subject was math. She also liked to read.

played the part of a girl with a brain aneurysm. She also landed a small role in the film *Human Nature*. She played a young version of Patricia Arquette's lead character. Hilary had to stretch as an actress for this role. She learned to cry on cue. Then she got what she thought was her big break. Hilary was cast in the pilot of a new television series called *Daddio*. She played one of the daughters of a stay-at-home dad. But before the television show aired, the producers decided that Hilary was not right for the part. They replaced her with another actress. Hilary was devastated and so discouraged about losing the part in *Daddio* that she did not know if she wanted to continue acting. She did not think she could face another audition. Hilary, Haylie, and Susan Duff went home to Texas. A few weeks later, Hilary's manager called and told her that the producers of a new Disney Channel television series wanted her to audition. Hilary said, "No, I don't want to do it, I'm done."[11] Disney called back and asked again, so Hilary read the script. That changed her mind. She and her mother thought the part was perfect for her. She decided to go to the audition.

The show was called *What's Lizzie Thinking*. Hilary was to try out for the lead role, a middle-school girl named Lizzie McGuire. The producers of the show wanted an actress who could portray a typical American girl. "We were looking for an average girl," said executive producer Stan Rogow. "She wasn't the cheerleader, she wasn't the diva, she wasn't the jock, she just was Lizzie."[12]

Hilary's first audition with Disney did not go well. "The casting director was like, 'You are totally unprepared. Do you know any acting coaches?'" said Hilary, "and I was like, 'Oh, my God!' I wanted to get under a rock and hide."[13] Over the next two weeks, the producers called Hilary back for several rounds of auditions. She had to read lines with other actors and perform in a variety of scenes. The show included an animated Lizzie who spoke the thoughts Lizzie McGuire could not say out loud. Hilary had to do a voice-over audition to make sure she could handle the double role of human Lizzie and cartoon Lizzie. She also had to show the producers any unique physical talents. At one audition, she walked on her hands around the room.

Hilary's personal style helped her land the role. "I kept wearing all these crazy outfits to the auditions," she said. "I identified with Lizzie. Lizzie McGuire was me— I was awkward, kind of clumsy."[14] The producers agreed. "She wasn't doing anything wrong," said Rich Ross, president of the Disney Channel's entertainment division. "She just wore such great outfits, and we wanted to see what she'd come in with next."[15]

Hilary Duff on the set of the Disney Channel's hit show *Lizzie McGuire* in 2001. Her role as the lovable and clumsy Lizzie launched Hilary into superstardom.

"Each time we saw Hilary, she was more interesting to watch," said Rogow. "So, while the auditioning process can be painful, part of what's revealed is who you're not getting bored with. Slowly, you began not to be able to take your eyes off Hilary. It became, 'That's the girl.'"[16]

If Hilary had been committed to work on *Daddio*, she would not have been available to play Lizzie McGuire. So, losing that part turned out to be a good thing. Besides, *Daddio* aired only a handful of episodes before NBC canceled the show.

Hilary won the role of Lizzie McGuire and signed a contract with Disney. It was the role that changed her life.

Suddenly a Star

Disney changed the name of Hilary's new television series to *Lizzie McGuire*. The first episode aired in January 2001. The show targeted the "tween" audience, viewers between the ages of eight and fourteen. Hilary and the character she played were both thirteen years old.

Hilary felt she had a lot in common with Lizzie. "If she was real, we'd be friends," she said.[1] She described her character as a normal girl. "She struggles through school, trying to fit in. She has embarrassing parents and an annoying little brother. And she just is kind of insecure and she's trying to find herself."[2] Hilary also admitted that, like Lizzie McGuire, she was a bit of a klutz. Disney capitalized on Hilary's ability to do physical comedy. She did her own stunts, and most episodes had Lizzie fall down, run into a locker, or get hit with something.

Lizzie McGuire showed viewers the challenges and mishaps of a typical middle-school girl. There were episodes about Lizzie's relationship with her family, her friends, school, and boys. Lizzie, with the help of her pals, Gordo and Miranda, survives picture day in a hideous unicorn sweater, a gift from her grandmother. She deals with her crush on the school heartthrob, Ethan, and an ongoing feud with snooty Kate Sanders. She faces the embarrassment of buying her first bra and kissing her first boy.

Middle-school students saw themselves in the characters and related to the show. Lizzie McGuire also appealed to younger viewers. They got a kick out of Lizzie's obnoxious little brother, Matt. "It's got something for everyone," said Hilary. "Girls like it because it's about them. Parents come up to me all the time and say they love it because it reflects their kids. The characters are easy to relate to."[3]

Lizzie McGuire combined live action with a sassy animated Lizzie. Animated Lizzie shared Lizzie's thoughts and fears with the audience. She said the things Lizzie was thinking but could not say out loud. Hilary had fun

Left to right: Lalaine Vergara-Paras as Miranda, Hilary Duff as Lizzie, and Adam Lamberg as Gordo in the children's TV series *Lizzie McGuire*.

matching her voice with the cartoon character. She often felt that she related more to animated Lizzie than to live Lizzie. "My cartoon character is a little more edgy and snappy," she said.[4]

Hilary felt at home on the kid-friendly *Lizzie McGuire* set. The cast was full of children her age and she enjoyed working with them. She also got along well with her TV parents, played by Hallie Todd and Robert Carradine. The cast became her second family. Several crew members brought their dogs to work, which suited animal-lover Hilary just fine. She found the easygoing, dog-filled set a perfect work environment.

A typical day for Hilary as the star of a television series began early. She woke up at 5:30 A.M. and was on the set by 7. The day was packed with wardrobe, hair and makeup, and script lines to practice. She also had three-and-a-half hours of school with a tutor. She shot scenes, did the voice-over for cartoon Lizzie, gave telephone interviews, and shot more scenes. After she finished on the set, Hilary went to voice lessons. Then she had homework to do and lines to learn for the next day.

Hilary also had responsibilities at home. She did chores and took care of her pets. Her hectic schedule left little time for relaxing or hanging out with friends. "My friends may want to have a sleepover, but I can't do it because I have to get up early the next day," she said. "But that's OK. I love what I do."[5]

Lizzie McGuire became a huge hit for Disney. More than 2.3 million viewers watched each episode. The show was the Disney Channel's highest-rated series for children ages six to fourteen. It was also the number-one show in its time slot. Entertainment critics loved Lizzie, and the show got great reviews. *Variety* called it "a clever and whimsical program."[6] Hilary Duff gained worldwide recognition and became a favorite of the

Lizzie Awards

In April 2002, Hilary Duff was nominated for the Favorite Television Actress award at the Nickelodeon Kids' Choice Awards. Although she did not win the award, the show in which she starred, *Lizzie McGuire*, was named Favorite Television Series. The show also received the Gracie Allen Award for its positive portrayal of girls and women.

tween crowd. She received some three hundred thousand letters a week as well as millions of e-mails from fans.

Hilary Duff was a celebrity. She found that her instant fame had its good points and its bad points. She enjoyed the opportunity it gave her to fly around the world and meet interesting people. And she liked the security of a steady role. On the other hand, Hilary sometimes missed her family after long days on the set. "The TV show does keep me away from my family," she said. "I don't get to see my dad much and my mom has to spend time away from my dad also and that's got to be hard, but they are very supportive."[7]

Fans recognized Hilary wherever she went and wanted to talk to her. She could not leisurely shop at the mall anymore because fans swarmed around her. She could not eat out at a restaurant without fans interrupting her meal to ask for her autograph. But Hilary kept a positive attitude and was willing to sacrifice a little privacy to do what she loved. "I have bad days, like everyone else," she said, "but I keep them in perspective and just wait for the sun to shine again."[8]

Disney looked for ways to capitalize on Hilary's popularity with teen viewers. In March 2002, she starred in *Cadet Kelly*, a Disney television movie. Hilary played the part of Kelly Collins, a free-spirited fourteen-year-old from New York. Kelly's life is turned upside down when her mother marries the commandant of a military school. Kelly has to move away from all she holds dear and is forced to attend her stepfather's military academy. The fun-loving girl who wore kooky fashions and pink lip gloss must learn to survive in the military world of structure and discipline.

Cadet Kelly was filmed in Toronto, Ontario, in Canada. Hilary enjoyed performing her own stunts, which included a military obstacle course and rifle training. She went through a week of intense military

A scene from the Disney Channel's 2002 movie *Cadet Kelly*. The title character, Kelly Collins, trades in her stylish clothes and fun hobbies for army fatigues and a military obstacle course. Hilary Duff attended boot camp for a week to prepare for the role.

training and a month of rifle drills to prepare for the role. "I had to learn how to throw rifles," she said. "I almost knocked myself out a few times!"[9] *Cadet Kelly* was a huge hit for the Disney Channel. It became the highest-rated original movie in the channel's history.

Lizzie McGuire remained hugely popular in its second and third seasons. Many famous actors and musicians made guest appearances on the show including pop star Aaron Carter, rock-and-roll legend Steven Tyler of Aerosmith, Frankie Muniz of *Malcolm in the Middle*, and Hilary's sister, Haylie.

Disney launched a merchandise campaign of *Lizzie* products. Clothing, accessories, cosmetics, video games, dolls, Frisbees, stickers, and stationery all carried *Lizzie* images. Disney Press published a best-selling series of *Lizzie McGuire* books with Hilary's picture on the covers. In August 2002, Disney released a *Lizzie McGuire* CD. Hilary sang an upbeat pop tune on the CD called "I Can't Wait." Later that year, she recorded a song on the *Disneymania* CD, which included such well-known singers as *NSYNC, Usher, and Christina Aguilera. They sang popular Disney tunes. Hilary's fans liked her singing and Disney decided to produce an entire CD for her. The CD was called *Santa Claus Lane* and contained a collection of Christmas songs. It did very well on the Billboard charts.

Hilary Duff

While Frankie Muniz and Hilary Duff worked together on an episode of *Lizzie McGuire*, Frankie told Hilary about a movie he was going to make. The film, *Agent Cody Banks,* called for a teenage girl. Frankie thought Hilary would be perfect for the role and suggested she audition. Hilary won the part and appeared in the spy/action movie with Frankie.

The lead singer of the rock band Aerosmith, Steven Tyler, and his daughter Chelsea guest starred in the 2002 Christmas episode of *Lizzie McGuire*.

The Billboard Charts

The Billboard charts are created by *Billboard* magazine. They list music sales and radio airplay for various categories of music.

Hilary played Natalie Connors, a scientist's daughter. Teen undercover CIA agent Cody Banks must get close to Natalie before her father's robot invention destroys the world. The problem is that Banks, who is fearless when it comes to protecting America, is a complete klutz around girls.

Hilary had fun working with her pal Frankie. They both had great comedic timing and added a lot of humor to the film. Hilary also enjoyed the nonstop action in the film and doing her own stunts. She got the chance to see firsthand how explosions and special effects were created in movies. She found the process fascinating. The tagline from the film, "Save the world. Get the girl. Pass math," summed up a plot that appealed to movie-goers of all ages.[10] The film was released in March 2003. It was another solid hit for Hilary.

Hilary finished filming the sixty-five episodes of her *Lizzie McGuire* contract. The series ended with Lizzie and her friends getting ready to graduate from middle school. Hilary agreed to play the part of Lizzie in a feature film called *The Lizzie McGuire Movie.* In the film, Lizzie and her classmates graduate from middle school and take a class trip to Rome, Italy. While sightseeing in Rome, Lizzie meets Paolo, one of Italy's biggest pop stars. Paolo mistakes Lizzie for his former partner, Isabella. The movie takes off from there. Handsome Paolo and starry-eyed Lizzie zip around Rome on Paolo's Vespa and Lizzie fills in for Isabella at a music awards show.

Hilary played two roles in *The Lizzie McGuire Movie*: blonde Lizzie and dark-haired Isabella. To play Isabella, Hilary had to learn to speak with an Italian accent. "Isabella is this very, very confident singer with big, crazy wild dark hair," said Hilary. "So it was a big change for me. And also she had an accent. So it was a little hard for me to do."[11] Hilary sang in the film and got to wear all kinds of high-fashion clothes.

Much of *The Lizzie McGuire Movie* was filmed in Rome. "It was amazing. I had never been to Europe before," said Hilary. "It was cool. We got to film at so many places: Trevi Fountain, the Coliseum, Spanish Steps . . . the main tourist attractions. The pizza was my favorite. I ate it like twice a day, every day."[12]

When Hilary filmed a movie, it was sometimes hard for her to be away from home. She took lots of pictures of her family and friends with her. She also brought along her favorite stuffed animal because it reminded her of home. "I go out of town a lot to make movies and I don't have my friends there, so I get a little lonely," she said. "But I like working, so it's kind of a tradeoff."[13]

The Lizzie McGuire Movie was released in May 2003. Hilary traveled all over the country to do publicity for the film. She appeared on *Good Morning America, Live with Regis and Kelly,* and *The Early Show.* She was nervous about whether or not the movie would be successful. It was her first starring role in a major motion picture. She knew that the film's success or failure rested

CD Sales

The Recording Industry Association of America (RIAA) certifies a CD gold when it sells five hundred thousand copies. A CD that sells one million copies is certified platinum. A CD that sells 10 million copies is certified diamond.

on her shoulders. Hilary had no need to fret. The film was a huge success. Disney also released a soundtrack of *The Lizzie McGuire Movie.* Hilary sang two songs on the CD. The album sold more than one million copies and was certified platinum.

Hollywood insiders wondered if Disney would carry the *Lizzie McGuire* series into the character's high-school years. They also discussed the possibility of making a sequel to the movie. "'Lizzie' was a great place to begin my career," said Hilary. "I loved the character, as it was very 'safe' for me, and doing the movie was a lot of fun."[14]

In a national survey, Hilary ranked as the most-popular female star with six- to eleven-year-old children. But some fans thought her name was Lizzie McGuire, not Hilary Duff. She did not want to be typecast as Lizzie forever. She wanted to branch out and try other roles. Hilary decided to end her involvement with *Lizzie McGuire* and focus her career on performing a variety of movie roles. She also had another dream. She wanted to be a singer.

Making Music

Hilary began to think about launching a singing career when she watched her sister, Haylie, rehearse with her band. She admired her sister's talent. She was also impressed by how Haylie was able to juggle singing and acting. Plus, it looked like a lot of fun!

Then Hilary attended a Radio Disney concert of young artists and decided she wanted to take the plunge herself. "There were all these pop acts backstage at the concert," she said. "They were all getting ready backstage and warming up, and I was like, 'I want to do this so bad.'"[1] Hilary met music producer Andre Recke at the concert. He agreed to work with her. "When I met

Hilary, I knew she had something special," said Recke. "Sometimes you just have that feeling, that, 'Wow, she's a star.'"[2]

Hilary developed a solid plan for achieving her goal. She took voice lessons and practiced for hours each day to strengthen her voice. She surrounded herself with music experts, producers, and songwriters. She worked with them to create the songs for her first CD. "Andre and I and my mom worked very hard to really get good music that I related to and was age-appropriate for me and wasn't just cheesy pop stuff," said Hilary.[3] She did all she could to make sure each song on her CD was perfect.

Hilary described her music as part pop, part rock. She named the CD *Metamorphosis*. The title, which is from the Greek language and means "a change in form," signified Hilary's new career path. Through her music, she hoped to distance herself from the character of Lizzie McGuire and establish herself in the minds of her fans as Hilary Duff. "Change is a very important and natural thing," she explained. "We called the album *Metamorphosis* because it's about changes that everybody experiences, especially kids. It's not just about me, but it is very personal."[4]

Hilary was excited about the CD because it enabled her to show her fans who she really was. Her roles in television and movies were designed by writers, directors, and producers. Her music was pure Hilary. "That's what is so cool about my music," she said. "It's more personal and it's more about me and I don't play a character, so I think that it is going to be nice to get people to know me better through my music."[5]

Making the transition from television and movie star to music star can be difficult. Hilary worried that her fans would not accept her as a singer. She feared they would not like her music. As the release date for her CD grew closer, Hilary's production team took her to meet some Top 40 radio programmers. They needed to convince the radio stations that her music would appeal to teens. Hilary and her team put in many long hours traveling to radio stations. They worked hard to make sure the stations played her songs.

Hilary's positive attitude and commitment to excellence convinced the radio executives. According to Abbey Konowitch, senior vice-president at Hollywood Records, Hilary was their biggest asset. "When we took her out to meet programmers, they were amazed with her poise, her smile, her passion about music and the fact she didn't look like the 12-year-old they were afraid she'd be," said Konowitch.[6]

Hilary released *Metamorphosis* in August 2003. It sold 204,000 copies its first week. It skyrocketed to number one on the charts in its second week of release.

By October, the CD had sold more than one million copies and was certified platinum. At fifteen years old, Hilary was the youngest artist to debut at number one in Canada. Five months after its release, *Metamorphosis* had sold more than three million copies and was certified triple platinum.

"So Yesterday" and "Come Clean" became hit singles off the album. Hilary combined music and acting to make music videos for the songs. She had fun making the videos and they became huge *Total Request Live (TRL)* requests on MTV. It was easy for Hilary to promote the song "So Yesterday" because she felt it had a good message for girls. The song encouraged girls to be independent. It reminded them that they did not need a boyfriend to be cool.

As Hilary neared her sixteenth birthday, she thought about the same thing most sixteen-year-olds think about—getting her driver's license. "I'm just obsessing about getting my license," she said. "That's all I think about. I'm counting down the days."[7]

Hilary's family surprised her with a birthday party in Kauai, Hawaii. She was scheduled to film a television music special on the island. Then she planned to relax with her family for a few days. She was thrilled when she stepped off the airplane and saw all of her friends waiting for her.

The television crew filmed *Hilary Duff's Island Birthday Bash*. Hilary and her family and friends celebrated in grand style. They danced the hula, explored caves, raced kayaks, surfed, and scuba-dived. They rode all-terrain vehicles over the beautiful landscape of the Kipu Ranch, sang songs around a campfire on the beach, and ate lots of coconut birthday cake.

As part of the music special, Hilary performed her first live concert at a party for her fans. She sang songs from her *Metamorphosis* CD. Since it was her first live concert, she was nervous. She feared she would forget the words to the songs or get the hiccups in the middle of a song. Performing live was a very different experience from performing on television and in movies where the director reshoots the scene if an actor flubs a line. "I'm used to being able to mess up and go again, and have no one see my mess-ups and have it not really matter," said Hilary. "But onstage you only have one shot and that made me nervous."[8]

Hilary gained courage from the audience. They knew the words to her songs, jumped up and down, and sang along with her. "The album had only been out for, like, four days, so I was so shocked that everybody knew the words," said Hilary. "It was great. Once I got up on stage, I got this huge rush of adrenaline, and all the scared inside me went away."[9]

Promoting a CD after its release is an important part of the music business. Hilary worked with her managers to plan her first concert tour. They had to choose which songs she would sing and the cities she would visit. Hilary spent long hours every day rehearsing with her band. She met with a wardrobe stylist and chose outfits and shoes for the tour. She practiced dance moves with a choreographer. "At first, I didn't know there was so much stuff involved and so many people involved in making an actual tour," said Hilary. "There are so many people with so many significant jobs that have to be done, that have to be finished, before we go on tour."[10]

Hilary was asked to sing at the American Music Awards (AMAs) show in November 2003. The show was a huge venue, watched by millions of people. Hilary had never performed live before such a large audience. She was so nervous that she could not sleep the night before the event.

Hilary rode to the AMAs in an SUV with her sister and her publicist. She greeted fans and gave an interview on the red carpet in front of the Shrine Auditorium in Los Angeles, California. Then she joined the musicians and celebrities backstage to get ready for her performance. Other performers that evening included Britney Spears, Rod Stewart, and Metallica.

Hilary wore all black for her performance, including knee-high black boots with four-inch heels. She sang two of her most popular songs: "Girl Can Rock" and "So Yesterday." Hilary ran around the stage, danced up stairs, and fell to her knees and swung her hair around. Her performance went off without a hitch, and she looked like a pro to the audience. "I did my show, and I was so nervous I thought I was going to throw up," she said afterward.[11] "It was the first time I felt like I had hit the big time, because I had to sing in front of all my peers."[12]

The day after the American Music Awards show, Hilary packed her bags and set out on tour. She traveled with a nine-piece band, her tour manager, and her production staff. The staff included sound people, a choreographer, and a wardrobe stylist. The team rode from one location to the next on a huge bus, complete with bunk beds, a living room, kitchen, bathroom, TVs, and games.

The tour lasted a month and included twenty cities. Hilary and her band started in Phoenix, Arizona, and made stops in Florida, New York, and California. The concerts sold out quickly and Hilary's popularity grew. She worked hard to conquer her fear of performing live. "Being on stage is totally different than acting in a movie or being on a TV show because it's all about yourself and

Hilary Duff rocks her performance on the 2003 American Music Awards.

how you want to act up there and the vibe that you want to give off," she said. "It's all up to you. You don't have a character hiding yourself."[13]

With each performance, Hilary's confidence grew. Her fans let her know that they accepted her as a singer and loved her music. They helped her overcome her fear of performing before a live audience. Their energy gave Hilary confidence as a singer. Even music critics praised her show. "She performs with a rock band," said Craig Bruck, Hilary's booking agent at Evolution Talent Agency. "It's not as poppy as you would think. It's an intense and exciting show."[14]

As much as Hilary enjoyed singing, she also loved to act. She decided that when the right acting roles came along, she would make time for both. In December 2003, she played a supporting role in the film *Cheaper by the Dozen*. She appeared with actors Steve Martin, who she described as "so funny!", Ashton Kutcher, "so cute!", and Tom Welling, "so nice!"[15] Hilary played Lorraine, the third-oldest child in a family with twelve children. Lorraine is popular in school, vain, and totally obsessed with fashion and makeup. "She thinks she should get more time in front of the mirror because she deserves it," said Hilary.[16]

Working on a comedy with twelve children meant that there was never a dull moment on the set. "If

Awards and More Awards

In April 2004, Hilary Duff accepted the award for Favorite Female Singer at Nickelodeon's 17th Annual Kids' Choice Awards in Los Angeles. The following month, she received the Today's Superstar award at the Young Hollywood Awards show. The award was given by *Hollywood Life* magazine to showcase emerging talent. Hilary also won the Best New Female Artist award at the 2004 World Music Awards.

someone makes a funny remark, all of us will start laughing and we can't control it," said Hilary. "We just keep laughing forever and they have to cut."[17] The fun they had making the film came through in the finished movie. *Cheaper by the Dozen* opened on Christmas Day 2003 and became a blockbuster hit.

In February 2004, Hilary joined fellow singers Ashanti and Usher as the musical headliners in the

National Basketball Association (NBA) All-Star Read to Achieve celebration. The event was part of the NBA all-star weekend. It was designed to help young people develop a lifelong love of reading and encourage adults to read regularly to children.

In the summer of 2004, Hilary set out on a summer concert tour. Her sister, Haylie, traveled with her and opened the show with a six-song set. They performed in California, the Midwest, and the East Coast. They also took the show to Canada. At a concert in Toronto, thousands of screaming fans chanted, "We want HIL-A-RY! We want HIL-A-RY!"[18] They waved glowsticks and homemade signs, danced in the aisles, and sang along with the music. Sometimes the enthusiasm grew so loud that Hilary's voice could not be heard over the din.

When Hilary and Haylie were not performing or practicing for a show, they filled in their free time helping others. In city after city, they visited sick children in local hospitals. Sometimes they passed out ice cream. Other times, they brought teddy bears to young patients. But mostly, they chatted with children, cheered them up, and took their minds off their illnesses. "It's good to know that you can give back," said Hilary, "and it makes you feel really good about yourself."[19]

Hilary took her music tour overseas. She sang in Australia, Japan, and Germany. One of the toughest

Hilary Duff accepts the award for Best New Female Artist at the 2004 World Music Awards in Las Vegas, Nevada.

things for Hilary about traveling around the world to perform was that she feared flying. She slept or watched movies to keep her mind off her fear. If the flight experienced turbulence, she prayed.

Hilary liked to keep busy and to have plenty of work. She always tried to give her fans her best performance, whether she was singing or acting. Sometimes, she felt pulled between the two careers. "I feel like I can't win with myself," she said. "I'll be in the middle of a tour and it's so fast-paced. It's like we're going here and there and we're in a new place every single night and then I'll get tired of it because I'm so exhausted. I'll be like, 'I wish I was filming a movie right now.' But then I'll be in the middle of filming a movie and I'll be bored and I'll be like, 'I wish I was on tour.'"[20] In spite of her hectic schedule and nonstop commitments, Hilary added another career to her already packed resume: entrepreneur.

Duff's Stuff

Hilary Duff learned how to sell products to teens when she played the role of Lizzie McGuire for the Disney Channel. Disney used Hilary's picture as Lizzie to sell everything from clothes to cosmetics. Now, Hilary began her own marketing campaign. She was the spokesperson for VideoNow, Hasbro's pocket-size video player. She also worked with a credit card company to create the Hilary Duff Visa Gift Card. The prepaid card was sold to tweens and teens. Hilary's picture was on the card, and teens could purchase cards in five different amounts from $25 to $200. According to Peter Klamka, the president of a marketing firm in

Michigan, "Hilary is responsible for $200 million in retail spending."[1]

Fans have always loved Hilary's unique fashion style. She wears all kinds of clothing, from vintage to designer and everything in between. Many of her fans wrote to Hilary and asked where they could buy clothes like hers. That gave her an idea—why not design a line of clothing for girls?

In the spring of 2004, Hilary launched Stuff by Hilary Duff. The product line included clothes, accessories, jewelry, furniture, cosmetics, and footwear. Stuff by Hilary Duff was sold at Target stores in the United States. It was also sold in Canada, Australia, New Zealand, and Europe.

Hilary played an active role in creating clothes that would make girls feel good about themselves. She wanted her designs to send the message that girls do not have to wear revealing clothes to be pretty or to fit in at school. "I don't dress for boys. I dress to feel cool and confident," she said. "Looking good and being trendy shouldn't mean showing a lot of skin, either."[2] Hilary's style advice was simple. "No matter how fashionable something is, only wear it if it looks good on you."[3]

Hilary helped pick out the colors, fabrics, and cut of the clothes in her collection. She helped design the hangtags. "Each of the product lines has a different theme," she said, "and I was involved in designing all of them—jeans, cute skirts, belts with chains, makeup, hair stuff, swimsuits, handbags, towels, and sheets, and everything! It was much harder than I thought."[4]

Stuff by Hilary Duff had leisure clothes, tracksuits, and T-shirts. There were rock-and-roll-themed pieces with slogans such as "Girlz Rock," "Awesome," and "Totally Cool." "When we made the fashion lines, we actually went into my closet," said Hilary. "We started drawing stuff and were, like, 'We like that. We hate that.'"[5] A good portion of the proceeds from her products goes to Hilary's charities. She also donates samples of her clothing to Kids With a Cause. KWAC gives the clothing to disaster victims, orphans, and needy children.

Hilary created a line of fashion dolls. There were three different versions: Hilary the Rock Star, Hilary the TV Star, and Hilary the Movie Star. All of the dolls' outfits and accessories were modeled after Hilary's own unique wardrobe.

Stuff by Hilary Duff sold so well that Hilary introduced a line of doggie clothes. The line was called Little Dog Duff Stuff. It was named after her favorite dog, Little Dog. The products included collars, leashes, and sweaters. All of the money from the sales of doggie products went to animal rescue groups.

Duff (center) poses with two models wearing outfits from her clothing line, Stuff by Hilary Duff, aimed at preteen and teen girls. The funky and age-appropriate attire is sold in Target stores.

Hilary's Likes and Dislikes

Hilary loves shoes. She has admitted that she owns more than one hundred pairs! She likes to wear shoes with heels—sometimes very high heels. "I *have* to check it out when I see a shoe store!" she said.[6]

Hilary loves funky jewelry. She also loves makeup and has lots of it. She once joked that her makeup will eventually need its own house.

She enjoys sushi, okra, pickles, and plain M&Ms. However, she does not eat eggs. She calls them "pre-life."

Hilary likes to read. "I never really liked reading until I found books that I really fell in love with," she said. "Since then I've been a reader. It expands your vocabulary and enables you to have conversations with people about things other than shopping and shoes."[7]

Hilary likes guys who are smart. She does not like guys who look like they spend more time in front of the mirror than she does.

At sixteen, Hilary got her driver's license. She also bought a Spanish-style mansion in Los Angeles, California. The six-bedroom house had a large pool, a big bright kitchen, and a custom-made mega-closet. Hilary furnished her new home with comfy couches, antique furniture, a grand piano, and a pool table. She lived with her mom. Her sister, Haylie, lived in a guesthouse on the property.

Hilary's love for animals prompted her to serve as youth ambassador for Return to Freedom. This nonprofit group is dedicated to preserving America's wild horses. Their goal is to keep wild mustang herds together and to give the horses a safe home. Hilary called the horses "national treasures." She worked to let people know that they were in danger of extinction. "It's so important to raise the awareness of other kids and that's the best part of being in the position I'm in," she said. "I think it's really important to give back to your community—and it makes you feel so good to get involved with a charity. I look up to people who are involved with organizations that help people and animals."[8]

Hilary visited the Return to Freedom ranch in California. She saw the most famous horse at the ranch, Spirit, the mustang that inspired DreamWorks' animated film *Spirit: Stallion of the Cimarron*. "I had to

Return to Freedom

Return to Freedom conducts educational programs for at-risk children and teens. Each program focuses on leadership, integrity, trust, and community within a group. Return to Freedom offers living history tours, where children play games, listen to stories, and learn about horses and herd behavior. There are also programs that teach children about the day-to-day operations of a ranch. Children help the ranch hands groom and feed the horses and burros. Some children camp overnight at the wild horse sanctuary.

catch my breath when I saw him," she said. "He's absolutely stunning."[9]

In July 2004, Hilary starred in *A Cinderella Story*. The film was a modern-day version of Cinderella but with a more girl-empowering message. Instead of waiting for her Prince Charming to sweep her off her feet,

Samantha Martin, the main character, works hard and fights for what she wants. The role was more dramatically complex than Hilary's previous roles. She had to use her imagination to create Samantha because nothing in Hilary's life remotely resembled Sam's. "It was really challenging," said Hilary. "All the projects that I've done I've been, like, really into clothes and hair and makeup and I've gotten to be a lot of who I am, and in this movie I had to totally build this character."[10]

Each movie provides unique challenges for its actors. In *A Cinderella Story*, Hilary had to learn to ballroom dance. In one scene, Hilary and costar Chad Michael Murray had to do an intricate waltz in a gazebo during filming. Hilary learned to dip and twirl in a princess ball-gown and high heels. The camera circled the gazebo as it filmed. Hilary and Chad had to rotate in a set pattern and hit specific points on the floor in time with the music and the camera.

Hilary worked hard to make her performance as Sam different from the other roles she had played. She hoped *A Cinderella Story* would appeal to an older audience. Hollywood Records released a soundtrack of the film. Hilary sang five of its fourteen songs. She and her sister, Haylie, recorded the song "Our Lips Are Sealed" for the CD. "We love working together," said Hilary of her sister. "We decided to do a version of 'Our Lips Are

Samantha (Hilary Duff) enters her school's Halloween dance in the modern-day version of the classic fairy tale, 2004's **A Cinderella Story.**

Sealed' because it's a good message for stuff that's going on in the movie and in my life, like dealing with gossip and all that high school drama."[11] The song talked about jealousy and the fact that spreading rumors was not cool. It encouraged teens to build each other up instead of tearing each other down.

A Cinderella Story did well at the box office, but most movie critics gave it a bad review. "This is a lame, stupid movie," wrote Roger Ebert in the *Chicago Sun-Times.*[12] Stephen Hunter of the *Washington Post* agreed. "They took the most famous tale in the world and broke it," he wrote.[13]

A week after the release of *A Cinderella Story*, Hilary went on a thirty-three-city summer concert tour. Her sister, Haylie, traveled with Hilary and opened the show. Hilary performed songs from her *Metamorphosis* CD and new songs. The popular single "Fly" was an audience favorite. The song encouraged teens to follow their dreams and never give up.

During the summer of 2004, Hilary faced a lot of negative press. Music critics belittled her singing. Movie critics said she could not act. She was also criticized for dating Joel Madden, the singer from the band Good Charlotte. Madden was covered with tattoos and was eight years older than Hilary. "There is absolutely no way you can prepare yourself for criticism," said Hilary, "and

I've had a lot of it recently. At first, everybody thought I was a joke for trying to become a pop star. Then certain people didn't like my music, and for some reason they didn't like the fact that I had my own clothing line. Suddenly, I seemed to be, like, the butt of all these jokes."[14]

Hilary realized that she could never please everybody. She could only please herself. The negative comments still hurt, but she tried not to dwell on them. "At first, when I got bad press, I would get really upset," she said. "But now it's just not worth my energy. People are going to say what they want to say. I can't change their minds."[15]

On September 28, 2004, her seventeenth birthday, Hilary released her second solo album, *Hilary Duff*. She named the CD after herself because she said it reflected the real Hilary. The songs were personal and reflected Hilary's experiences of the past year. "The music is more 'me' than the acting," she said. "And the second album is so much cooler! It's very rock. Some of it's punky, but it's not too edgy. I just can't wait for people to hear it because they'll totally understand it and who I'm talking about and how I'm feeling inside."[16]

Hilary carefully chose each song for the CD. She often talked about how music can lift her spirits. She worked hard to make sure her music did that for her fans. "I think the album has more depth to it," she said.

"As I keep going forward, the music will keep growing up with me."[17]

Hilary and her sister, Haylie, wrote three of the songs on the CD. The song "Haters" was Hilary's response to the "mean girl" trend. The song took aim at mean-spirited gossip, envy, greed, and jealousy. Hilary made it clear on the song that she did not agree with the idea that it was cool for girls to be mean and belittle each other. She felt that girls could relate to the song because it talked about the kinds of behaviors common in many high schools.

Bob Cavallo, chairman of the Buena Vista Music Group, was impressed by Hilary's new CD. He also admired Hilary's ability to juggle music, acting, philanthropy, and a business empire. He found her calm attitude amazing in the midst of her whirlwind life. "Sure, she's cute and wholesome," he said, "but she is also talented, intelligent, essentially decent and humble. You put those things together, along with incredible focus, and that really is something special."[18]

Hilary loved making music and touring with her band. She also wanted to continue acting. She looked for dramatic roles in addition to the comedy roles for which she was famous. "Since I'm getting older, it's hard to find parts that are wholesome," she said. "I know

I can handle dramatic roles, but I don't think I should have to play a young mother on crack to prove it."[19]

In October 2004, Hilary starred in the film *Raise Your Voice.* The film allowed her to combine singing and acting. She played the role of Terri Fletcher. Terri wants to be a singer and attend a summer music program in Los Angeles. Her dream is cut short by her overprotective father and a family tragedy. "This role is definitely more dramatic, which is a good step for me," explained Hilary. "I've been playing the girl next door, but I want to do other things."[20]

Hilary had to cry on cue for the role, which she said was not that difficult. She thought the biggest acting challenge was showing Terri's reaction to tragedy. Hilary had to show Terri without emotion—a girl without happiness, without sadness, completely numb and closed-off to the world around her. Eventually, though, Terri overcomes many obstacles and regains her self-confidence and love of singing. *Raise Your Voice* was Hilary's favorite film, but it was a box office flop.

On December 26, 2004, a giant tsunami hit Southeast Asia. It was one of the deadliest natural disasters in history. Thousands of people were killed and millions left homeless in eleven countries. Hilary donated a portion of the ticket sales from her concert tour to help the victims and their families. She also helped raise money to rebuild a school in India. "I, just like everyone else, have watched this terrible tragedy and feel so sorry for the children and the families who have lost so much!" she said.[21]

In January 2005, Hilary took her band to Canada. She performed to sold-out crowds of screaming fans. She also agreed to act in several movies and began to plan her next CD. "I do love my job, really I do, despite all the pressures and the stress," she said. "I don't want to become one of those child stars who fades into obscurity the moment they turn 20. I've got plans and ambitions, and if anything, I want to become even more famous than I am now. And I am prepared to work for it."[22]

Doing It All

In January 2005, Hilary Duff performed at President George W. Bush's Inaugural Youth Concert in Washington, D.C. She sang "Fly," a song from her second CD. She dedicated the song to the men and women of the military. She chose the song because she wanted to encourage the troops. The lyrics urged them to trust themselves and never give up. Her performance was a huge hit with the ten thousand fans in the audience, but Duff had an embarrassing moment at the event. When she and President Bush tried to high-five each other, they missed.

Duff looked for ways to expand her career and keep it moving forward. She wanted to keep her young pre-teen fans. But she also wanted to broaden her appeal and become more popular with young adults. In early 2005, Duff added Robert Thorne to her management team. Thorne had guided the careers of Mary-Kate and Ashley Olsen to a billion-dollar empire. Thorne focused on Duff's retail career. She also had managers to help direct her music and acting careers.

In June 2005, Duff helped kick off National Military Families Week in Washington, D.C. The event was sponsored by the Armed Forces Foundation to show support for U.S. troops and their families. Duff read to children of U.S. soldiers fighting in Iraq and Afghanistan. She also signed autographs and posed for pictures with her fans. Duff supports the troops because they are "helping our country and keeping our freedom and our liberty. So any little thing that I can do to give back, I want to be a part of it," she said.[1]

Duff often gives free concert tickets for her shows to military families. She also visits injured soldiers at the National Naval Medical Center in Bethesda, Maryland. "Their stories are incredible," she said. "Who knows if they even care about me, but I think it's that I come that's important. When there are people who are 19 years old, putting their life on the line fighting for our freedom every single day, you should support them. Show them that respect."[2]

Duff's next film, *The Perfect Man,* was released in June 2005. Hilary played the part of Holly Hamilton. What attracted her to the role was the fact that Duff was nothing like Holly. "I think that when I read the script what I liked the most about it is that I don't relate to her at all," said Duff. "The only thing I had in common with Holly is that we both liked eyeliner, a lot of it."[3]

Duff called the film a great mother/daughter movie. The plot centered around the relationship between Holly and her mom, Jean. Played by Heather Locklear, Jean bounces from one bad relationship to another. She makes poor choices and each relationship eventually fails. When that happens, Jean uproots Holly and her sister and they move to a new city. Holly is tired of having her life turned upside down every time her mom breaks up with a man. She tries to find her mom the perfect man so that she will stay put for a while. When she cannot find one, Holly makes one up. She uses the Internet to make her plan believable, and her mother falls for a made-up Mr. Right.

The Perfect Man did not do well at the box office. Most critics did not like the film or Hilary Duff's performance. "*The Perfect Man* is so imperfect that it may qualify as one of the summer's worst movies," wrote

Hilary Duff reads to children of U.S. troops fighting in the Middle East during National Military Families Week in 2005.

Claudia Puig in *USA Today*.[4] Stephen Hunter of the *Washington Post* agreed. "Not to be too rough on one so young, but it's hard to see a single thing about the pleasant but eminently forgettable Duff that makes her so essential to today's Hollywood."[5] Even though the bad reviews stung, Duff tried not to let them bother her. "The 50-year-old person that's writing the review is not who is meant to see my movie," she said. "I don't care what they think of the movie. They're 50."[6]

In August, Duff released her third CD, *Most Wanted*. She called the album a collection of her favorite songs.

Music from her first two CDs was remixed so that it sounded different. Duff also cowrote three new songs for the album with her boyfriend Joel Madden and his brother Benji. Duff worked hard to give her fans a CD they would enjoy. She pushed herself and those around her to strive for excellence. "She's a workhorse," said Benji. "I was like, 'Can we take a break? We've been singing for nine hours, girl!'"[7]

Duff experimented with new sounds on *Most Wanted*. She wanted to give her fans a taste of what they would hear on her concert tour. "Wake Up has a very pop, dancy kind of '80s vibe to it," she said, "and we did another song called Beat Of My Heart that sounds kind of techno. And we did a song called Break My Heart that's more pop-punk-rock-sounding . . . it's just all different and each song has a totally different vibe to it."[8]

Duff traveled around the country to promote *Most Wanted*. She appeared on *The Tonight Show With Jay Leno, Today, TRL,* and *Access Hollywood.* Her hard work paid off. The album sold close to 208,000 copies its first week and was Billboard's top-selling CD. It stayed the number-one album in the country for a second week. Then sales dropped off sharply. Although the CD sold more than one million copies and was certified platinum, it did not do as well as Duff's earlier albums.

Duff and her band began their *Still Most Wanted* tour in the United States to promote the CD *Most Wanted*. She began with a concert in Los Angeles, California, and traveled to Denver, Chicago, Miami, and many cities in between. She had fun rocking out at her shows, but her enthusiasm took its toll on her teeth. In one small town, she had to make an emergency visit to a dentist. "My teeth aren't the strongest," she said, "and I kept chipping them on the microphone. One show, I literally spit half of my two front teeth out."[9] She found a local dentist, had her two front teeth bonded, then worked the rest of the day.

On August 29, 2005, Hurricane Katrina struck the gulf coast of Louisiana and Mississippi. The storm caused billions of dollars worth of damage. Thousands of people were left homeless. Duff donated $250,000 to help the victims of the disaster. "It's heartbreaking to see the devastation on TV," she said. "People are missing family members, and they have absolutely nothing left, not even food or water. I want to do everything I can to help those who have survived to help rebuild their lives."[10] Duff asked her fans to bring as many canned goods to her concerts as they could carry. Some fans brought carloads of food. Together, they collected more than 4 million pounds of canned goods. Duff donated the food to USA Harvest. They sent it to the people in need.

Hilary Duff greets a student in New Orleans on August 29, 2006, the one-year anniversary of Hurricane Katrina. Duff donated a quarter of a million dollars to the relief effort. With the help of her fans, she also collected millions of pounds of food for the victims of the disaster.

Hilary Duff turned eighteen in September 2005. She began to talk openly about her relationship with Good Charlotte singer Joel Madden. She admitted that although he was eight years older, they complemented each other and shared the same values. "I like someone that's kind of like an undercover dork," she said. "I'm like an undercover dork. Someone who thinks the lifestyle we lead is funny."[11] Neither of them liked to party until the wee hours of the morning. They preferred quiet evenings at home hanging out with friends. "In some magazines, they almost want me to deny what I am, and I never do that because I really am comfortable with myself," said Duff. "I am a good girl. I'm not going to try to prove to anybody else that I'm not this clean-cut type of person, because I am. I'm not crazy out there partying all the time."[12]

Like other celebrities, Hilary Duff often has photographers follow her when she shops or runs errands. One tabloid reporter snapped an unflattering picture on her day off. The picture was printed in the tabloid, plastered under the headline, "Duff Puffs." The article made fun of her weight and called her fat. Duff became self-conscious about her body. She felt pressured to lose weight. She decided to exercise and get into shape.

Her best friend, Taylor, was traveling with her on her music tour and joined Duff in her new fitness program. They swam thirty laps a day. They also did Pilates. Duff cut pasta, rice, and bread out of her diet. "I've made myself be really good for the last couple of months," she said. "I used to be obsessed with French fries. Like I'm the biggest French fry person in the world. I could eat French fries all day."[13] Duff also changed how often

Good Charlotte lead singer Joel
Madden and Hilary Duff attend the
2005 American Music Awards in Los
Angeles, California. Despite their
eight-year age difference, they got
along well and both avoided the wild
Hollywood lifestyle that got many of
their peers in trouble.

she ate. Instead of three meals a day, Duff ate a little bit throughout the day. She did not feel hungry, had plenty of energy, and was able to change her body to a leaner look.

Hilary Duff was happy with her new appearance, but she was still self-conscious about her body. She continued to lose weight. At one point, she got too thin. Tabloids hinted that she had an eating disorder. Her sister, Haylie, helped her to develop good eating habits and maintain a healthy weight. "I'm just a normal girl," said Hilary. "Some days I think I'm beautiful, and other days I think there is nothing that can help me."[14]

In September 2005, the California School Nutrition Association launched a fitness program for children. Their slogan, "Stay fit. Eat right. Looking good, California!" encouraged young people to eat healthy foods and get plenty of exercise.[15] Because of her experience with weight issues, Hilary Duff helped promote the program. She read public service announcements on the radio to inspire children to eat healthy foods, be active, and have fun.

After she finished her U.S. concert tour, Hilary Duff took her band to Australia. Her concerts sold out quickly and got great reviews. When she was in Australia, the family of a young fan contacted her with a request. Their son, eight-year-old William Styles, had recently died

One of the Beautiful People

Hilary Duff was named one of *People* magazine's fifty most-beautiful people in 2005. She was also named one of *Teen People*'s hottest stars under the age of twenty-five. *Forbes* magazine listed Duff in their "Celebrity 100" list. The list reports the top one hundred celebrities by their earnings from entertainment income. Later that year, Duff was given *CosmoGirl*'s "Born to Lead" award. The award is given annually to recognize celebrities who make a positive impact with their lives.

of leukemia. William had been a huge Hilary Duff fan. Before he died, William asked his family to contact Duff if she ever came to Australia. He wanted her to visit the sick children at Westmead Children's Hospital.

Duff met with William's family. She visited Westmead Children's Hospital, brought gifts for the sick children, and spent an afternoon talking with them. Since these children were too sick to attend one of her concerts, Duff gave them each a special memory—not of rock bands and flashing lights, but a memory straight from her heart. She showed them she cared.

In December 2005, Hilary Duff appeared in *Cheaper by the Dozen 2*. The sequel brought the Baker family back for a look at a family vacation with twelve children. The gang rented a rustic cabin on Lake Winnetka. They competed against their rivals, the Murtaughs, a family with eight children, in a Labor Day competition. Once again, most critics did not like the film or Duff's performance. But the movie earned millions at the box office.

Hilary Duff took a few weeks off to celebrate Christmas and New Year's with her family. She enjoyed the slower pace and the chance to catch up with old friends over the holidays. By early January 2006, she was ready to get back to work. She packed her bags and headed to Canada, Europe, India, and Mexico to continue her *Still Most Wanted* tour.

A Year of Changes

Hilary Duff's concerts sold out quickly and got great reviews. After one show in London, James Reaney of the London Free Press wrote, "Duff has the stuff to last a while, a long while as an entertainment force."[1] As always, Duff made time to serve others while on tour. She visited a homeless shelter in downtown Edmonton, Alberta, as part of her campaign to raise awareness about poverty and hunger. She served chicken and stew to hundreds of homeless people at the shelter.

Duff traveled back to her home state in March 2006 to sing at the Houston Rodeo. "I was shocked when they asked me, because it's the biggest deal in Houston," she said.[2] Duff was thrilled to be back in Texas and broke attendance records for her concert. More than seventy-two thousand people watched her perform.

August 2006, the first anniversary of Hurricane Katrina, was a busy month for Hilary Duff. She went to Louisiana to help out. She visited Camp Hope, Louisiana, a home for volunteers who were working to clean up the gulf coast. Duff served meals to the volunteers. She also went to New Orleans to provide dinners to those in need through USA Harvest. She donated more than 207,000 meals to people who still needed them to survive. "Working with other volunteers and meeting people who truly need help taught me that hunger and poverty can happen to anyone," said Duff. "I'm lucky to be in a position where I can spread the word, but you don't have to be famous to do something. Anyone can give their time or donate canned food that's just sitting in their cupboard—it really makes a difference."[3]

That same month, Hilary Duff released another movie. Hilary, her sister, Haylie, and their mom, Susan Duff, produced the film *Material Girls*. Hilary and Haylie starred in the movie. They played rich, spoiled, cosmetic company heiresses. The sisters love their fancy house and expensive cars. Shopping is their favorite activity. When their father dies and a scandal surrounds

Haylie (left) and Hilary Duff play snooty heiresses who lose everything and must learn to work hard for a living in the 2006 riches-to-rags story *Material Girls*.

his cosmetics company, the girls fall on hard times. They lose all of their possessions and must learn how to do things like wash dishes, ride a bus, and apply for a job.

Hilary enjoyed working with Haylie. "We are so close and always have been," she said. "It's nice to have her to talk to when I feel like my friends or my boyfriend or my mom don't understand."[4] Hilary calls Haylie her role model. "She is so talented and inspiring to me," said

Hilary of her sister. "She is an amazing young woman with inner strength that I see daily. . . . Haylie is the best big sister a girl could have."[5]

As much as she enjoyed working with her sister, Hilary Duff did not like working with the four-legged members of the cast. She has always loved dogs—she has five of them! But Duff is not crazy about cats. "We did this scene in a house with a lot of cats, and it was disgusting," she said. "Cats freak us out a little, like how someone who didn't grow up with dogs is weirded out by them. We had cat hair stuck to our lip gloss, all over our clothes, just . . . yuck! It was so gross."[6]

Critics did not care for *Material Girls* and the film did not earn much at the box office. Hilary and Haylie were nominated for Razzie Awards for their performances. Razzies are given for the worst performances of the year.

In the fall of 2006, Hilary Duff teamed with cosmetics giant Elizabeth Arden to release her own perfume. She named the fragrance "With Love . . . Hilary Duff." She wanted the perfume to be "an expression of love in all its forms: the unconditional love of family, the generosity of friendship and the breathtaking excitement of romance."[7] Duff said the fragrance captured two sides of her personality: her fun, spirited side, but also her sophisticated side. She described the scent as a cross

"A Hidden Gem"

Many celebrities create fragrances. They are designed to be perfume versions of their personalities. Fragrance experts analyze, judge, and critique the perfumes. Most of the fragrances do not hold up well to expert scrutiny. "With Love . . . Hilary Duff" was an exception. Hannah Sandling, TV presenter, writer, and stylist gave the fragrance four stars out of five. "This perfume is a hidden gem," she said. "Wearing it made me feel more confident and sent me into a dreamy state, as though I was in an exotic location."[8]

between something sexy and sweet. She helped design the packaging for the perfume. She used the colors of her bedroom, blue and purple, for the box. She also used clips from one of her music videos in ads to promote the fragrance. "With Love . . . Hilary Duff" ranked number three in department store fragrance sales.

In October, Duff experienced a negative aspect of fame. Two men, a nineteen-year-old Russian immigrant

Hilary Duff makes an appearance at Macy's Herald Square in New York City September 14, 2006, to promote her perfume.

and his roommate, began stalking her. One of the men, Maksim "Max" Myaskovskiy, claimed he came to the United States to be with Duff. He thought they belonged together and promised to remove anyone who stood in his way. He threatened to harm Duff and her boyfriend, Joel Madden.

Hilary Duff feared for her life. She also feared Myaskovskiy would hurt her loved ones. She filed a restraining order against the two men to prevent them from getting within one hundred feet of her. The obsessed fan was arrested, convicted of stalking, and sentenced to 117 days in jail.

Later that month, Duff and her beloved Chihuahua Lola made their debut as video game characters in the video game, The Sims 2 Pets. "Although she's trying not to let it go to her head, Lola is very excited to make her cameo in The Sims 2 Pets," said Duff.[9] Duff's video game character played with Lola, browsed some shops, and chatted with other Sims characters.

In December, Mattel released the Red Carpet Glam Hilary Duff Barbie Doll. To get the doll to match her proportions, Duff had to stand in a machine that digitally scanned her body. The twelve-inch doll was sold with Duff wearing a black-and-white polka-dot dress and a red satin sash. Duff helped design eleven different head-to-toe outfits for her Barbie. Some she called sweet and others she labeled rocker.

Hilary Duff's sister, Haylie, and her four dogs moved into Hilary's Los Angeles home. Susan Duff moved to a house a few doors down the street. Hilary enjoyed the independence of living on her own without her parents. But she still maintained a close relationship with her mom. They talked on the phone several times a day. They shared meals and cooked together. They sometimes stayed overnight at each other's homes.

By the end of 2006, Hilary Duff and her boyfriend, Joel Madden, had broken up. They had been dating for two and a half years. Also, Duff's parents filed for divorce. It was an emotionally draining, difficult time for Hilary Duff. She kept her feelings to herself and did not talk publicly about her personal life. She did not want anyone to know about her problems. "I was embarrassed that my family wasn't perfect," she said.[10]

Duff's situation was made more difficult by the constant attention she received from the press. "It's like, we can't be normal people anymore," she said, "because people always watch what we're doing and you can never show how you feel because if you have one bad day or you don't feel like smiling and being all bubbly and energetic, you read in the paper the next day what a brat you are."[11]

Hilary Duff poured all of her energy into her career. She read scripts and considered new acting roles. She kept a notebook and worked on ideas for new songs. Her strong work ethic and healthy self-respect kept her moving forward.

Dignity

Hilary Duff was becoming a young woman. She did not want her career to fade away like the careers of many child stars. She loved acting and making music and wanted to continue doing both for a long time. But many people in the entertainment business still thought of her as cute little Lizzie McGuire. Bad movie reviews and casting directors who would not hire her for any role other than the girl next door added to her problem. She had to find a way to play more mature roles and appeal to an older audience.

Duff decided to take a break from acting until the right role came along. She was still offered scripts to read, but she turned them down if she did not think they would move her career forward. She focused on her music and business empires. She wrote songs for her next CD. She attended fashion shows in New York to keep up with the latest fashion trends.

In February 2007, Hilary Duff unveiled the latest styles for her children's clothing line. Duff's clothes were modeled at *Child* magazine's Fall Fashion Show during New York's Fashion Week. It was the first runway show for Duff's fashion collection. Sixty-seven children modeled a variety of styles from various designers, including Duff. Mayan Lopez, daughter of comedian George Lopez, was one of the girls who wore an outfit from Stuff by Hilary Duff. "I try to make it cool and cutting-edge like something I would wear," said Duff of the new line, "but also more embellished and colorful because it is for girls."[1]

Duff expanded her Stuff by Hilary Duff line to include clothes for teens as well as tweens. "I like to try different things and have fun," she said. "I know guys can do it too, but it is so much fun to be a girl and play around with so many looks. Every day I'm inspired to try something new that I see in a magazine. You know, dream up an idea and wear my clothes different ways. I like being able to express myself through my clothes."[2]

Stuff by Hilary Duff offered tweens and teens an inexpensive way to share Duff's casual yet chic style.

Duff released a line of McCall's sewing patterns for children's clothes. Parents can use the patterns, select their own fabrics, and make stylish outfits for their children. The finished outfits cost a fraction of the price of store-bought clothing. Duff believed the patterns provided children the chance to wear unique clothes and not have to worry about seeing their outfit worn by several others at school.

She also created a line of craft accessories that teens can use to customize their clothes. The line included charms, stones, patches, and iron-on graphics. According to Duff, the new line "allows you to get creative with your style—so you can always wear something new to highlight your own individuality."[3] Hilary Duff also participated in a Web site called Stardoll. Fans select their favorite from a list of celebrities and then choose clothes to dress them in their unique style. The site is a modern-day version of paper dolls. After the celebrities are dressed in cool clothes, users can place them in different virtual scenes.

In addition to her fashion lines, Duff found a creative way to keep her music in the ears of her fans. In March 2007, she teamed up with Tiger Electronics, a division of Hasbro, to promote a musical toothbrush. The idea was to get children to brush their teeth for a full two minutes. That is the amount of time generally recommended by dentists to provide a thorough brushing. Each tooth-brush held a single chip of music embedded in the handle. Children could choose a Hilary Duff song, or select a tune from another of their favorite artists. The Tooth Tunes toothbrush sent sound waves through the bristles. They traveled through the jawbone to the inner ear where the child heard the music. Each music clip played for two minutes.

Duff liked to stay in touch with her fans. Through a blog on her Web site, she let her fans know what was going on in her life. She wrote blog entries between concerts, on airplanes, and on movie sets. She shared

One of the Top Earners

Hilary Duff was a shrewd businesswoman, and her marketing strategies were very successful. In 2007, *Forbes* magazine esti-mated Duff's yearly earnings at twelve million dollars and ranked her number seven of the twenty top-earning young superstars.

pictures from her travels and from her concerts. She often asked her fans' opinions on what songs or videos they liked best. She listened to them and made them part of her decision making. "I am going to rely on you guys to tell me what you like from clothing to wallpaper to ringtones to podcasts," she wrote. "So, stay involved because I really value your opinion!"[4]

Hilary Duff released *Dignity*, her fourth CD, in April 2007. She chose the title *Dignity* because she felt the conduct and speech of many Hollywood celebrities did not reflect the trait. She wanted to encourage her fans to maintain a healthy self-respect regardless of their surroundings. "Dignity is something that my mom has always really tried to instill in my sister and I," she said, "and it's not something that you can be given or that you can just get or you were born with. It is something that you have to work on. It's not always the easiest road to take, but it's something that I hope to always strive to have."[5]

Duff cowrote all but one of the fourteen songs on *Dignity*. The album was very personal to her. The songs talked about things that were going on in her life. She wrote about the sadness she felt over the breakup of her parents' marriage. She wrote about her relationship with Joel Madden and the loneliness she felt when they stopped dating. She wrote about the fear and anger she felt as the victim of a stalker. She also wrote about the vanity of Hollywood and how many of its stars are completely self-absorbed. "It is a dance record, but I wanted it to be serious," she said. "I wanted to talk about serious things, but do it in a not-so-serious way, with music that makes you want to get up and dance."[6]

Duff found writing music therapeutic, yet stressful. It was a way for her to work through some painful issues. On the other hand, it was difficult for her to open up and show her deepest feelings to the world. She decided that many people deal with loss and sadness. Through her music, she could help not only herself, but she could also help her fans. "I wanted the album to be honest," she said. "I'm not perfect, and I don't have a perfect family. This album lets people inside my life—not the life everybody thinks they know or that they read about, but my real life."[7]

Dignity entered at number four on the Billboard charts its first week. It sold more than 140,000 copies. Music critics liked the CD and gave it positive reviews. They thought it had a more mature sound than Duff's previous albums. "She's never sounded less eager to please or more messily human," said music critic Jonathan Bernstein. "On the evidence of *Dignity*, heartache brings out the best in her."[8] The single "With Love" was a fan favorite. It hit the number-one spot on the Commercial Pop Chart.

Duff promoted *Dignity* on *Good Morning America, Jimmy Kimmel Live,* and *The Ellen DeGeneres Show.* "No matter how the album sells, I am proud of it because it came from my heart!" she said.[9] In June 2007, she traveled to Toronto for the MuchMusic Video Awards Show. She won the People's Choice Favorite International Artist award. She also hosted the Teen Choice Awards. "With Love" won the award for Choice Music: Love Song.

In July 2007, Hilary Duff and her band began the first leg of her *Dignity* summer concert tour in Canada. She danced choreographed routines with backup dancers for the first time on the tour. It was a new challenge for her because she was not a professional dancer. But, as with all of her goals, Duff worked hard and mastered the steps. "Because you guys supported me so much during my last tour," she told her fans, "I want to make sure that I have a new exciting show for you. Things that you have never seen me do before. New show. New band. New look. New everything."[10]

Duff's *Dignity* tour continued with concerts in the United States, Mexico, Brazil, and Australia. An older crowd attended the shows. She had always had young girls and their moms in the audience for her concerts. Now, she saw teens—older teens who did not bring their

Duff performs with her backup dancers on NBC's *Today* show in 2007 to promote her fourth album, *Dignity*. Her tour featured choreographed routines, a first for the actress/singer.

parents along. Even though it cut Duff's ticket sales in half, she was happy her music appealed to older teens. Just as she was growing, she wanted her fans to grow with her.

Duff performed the same songs in the same order night after night on tour. Sometimes the act started to feel a bit stale to her and her band. To spice things up and keep everyone on their toes, they played tag. On-stage. During the concert. They did it subtly, as a way to keep the show fresh and exciting. The audience did not even know they were playing a game.

As on her earlier tours, Duff spent her free time working for her favorite charities. She served meals at homeless shelters in Canada. In Louisville, Kentucky, she helped collect more than half a million meals for USA Harvest.

A Bright Future

Hilary Duff began dating professional hockey player Mike Comrie in 2007. "He's funny, and I like that," she said. "And of course I'm attracted to him! I love men who have a lot going on in their lives, like I do."[1] Comrie surprised Duff with a Mercedes-Benz SUV for her twentieth birthday on September 28, 2007.

Throughout her career, Duff has been labeled a "good girl." The description fits. She does not hang out at clubs night after night and dance on tables. She has never been arrested for alcohol or drug abuse. She has never spent time in a rehab facility. Duff takes her responsibility as a role model to her fans seriously.

She believes it is important to set a good example in her personal life. "I've had a lot of help from people," she said. "It's a joint effort with my family and everyone helping me balance my life."[2]

Many people felt Duff's healthy lifestyle was a refreshing change from that of many former child stars who spin out of control when they near adulthood. Because Duff handled the transition with apparent ease, she was featured in the book *The Key: Celebrated People Unlock Their Secrets to Life* by Linda Solomon. The photojournalist, a longtime key collector, took black-and-white photographs of all sorts of keys. Then she

Oh, So Neat

Hilary Duff travels a great deal and is away from home for long stretches of time. When she gets the chance to hang out at home, Duff keeps her house neat and tidy. "I'm OCD when it comes to cleaning," she said. "I can't go to bed with a messy room. That would totally wig me out. It freaks me out to have dishes in the sink."[3]

asked fifty-four celebrities to share their key words of wisdom. Solomon paired each celebrity quality with a key photograph that represented that quality. A portion of the book's proceeds went to breast cancer research.

The book's celebrities included actor Sidney Poitier, comedian Tim Allen, and golf pro Tiger Woods. Sidney Poitier shared the key to character. Tim Allen shared the key to laugher, and Tiger Woods shared the key to winning. Hilary Duff shared the key to staying grounded. "Our home chores were the thing that always kept it real for us," she said. "We had to help with dinner chores every night, keep our rooms neat, and take care of our pets. We also were taught to share and to volunteer our time from an early age."[4]

In May 2008, Duff found the perfect role to jump-start her acting career. She appeared in the dark comedy *War, Inc.* The movie is set in the fictional nation of Turaqistan. It tells the story of a war fought and managed by private defense contractors. The film was meant to cause viewers to question the political power of global corporations in the Iraq war. The star, John Cusack, helped write and produce the film. He wrote Duff's role specifically for her.

Duff played Yonica Babyyeah, a foul-mouthed, spoiled pop star who gets caught in an assassin's scheme. It was her first R-rated movie. "I was a little nervous," she said. "Because Yonica really isn't like how I am in real life. It's a real stretch, totally different from anything that anyone's ever seen me do before. In fact, she's kind of everything that I stand against. Which was really fun to get to play. But it also gets to prove a point, to show how she represents this sort of over-sexed, overdone image that's sold to young people—to young girls—and makes them think, 'Oh, that's how I should be.'"[5] Academy Award winners Ben Kingsley and Marisa Tomei appeared in the movie along with Dan Aykroyd and Joan Cusack.

Duff flew to Bulgaria where the movie was filmed and worked on creating a believable accent. She dyed her hair black and plastered on heavy makeup. For the first time in her acting career, she had to shoot a machine gun in a movie. She also had to use bad language and dress in more revealing clothes than she had ever worn in a film. John Cusack liked Duff's performance so much he asked her to star in his next film. "She's a great actress," said Cusack. "I just spent the entire fall with her and she was a revelation every day. I don't think people know that yet, but they're gonna."[6] Most film critics did not like the film, but Duff's performance got rave reviews.

Many people wondered if Duff's role in an R-rated movie would bother her longtime fans. Duff hoped not, but she purposely took the role to expand her career. She wanted to play someone other than the young, sweet

A dark-haired Hilary Duff as the sultry songstress Yonica Babyyeah in 2008's *War, Inc.* This role was very different from anything Duff had played before, and critics praised her performance.

girl next door. "I'm growing up," she said, "and my fans are going to grow up with me. I think there will be a mixed emotion about it. But if I lose fans, well, I don't want to limit myself in my career."[7]

Duff was expanding her career, but she had not abandoned her young fans. Her next film, a computer-animated family comedy, appealed to a younger audience. *Foodfight!* tells the story of what happens in a grocery store at night when the store closes and the produce comes to life. Duff provided the voice of Sunshine Goodness, the girl on a box of raisins. Hilary's sister, Haylie, as well as Charlie Sheen, Wayne Brady, and Eva Longoria Parker supplied the voices of the other main characters.

Hilary Duff's acting career was picking up speed. In 2008, she filmed three movies. In the drama *Greta*, she played the title role, a teenager who is trying to find meaning in her life. "The character's obsessed with suicide," said Duff. "She's funny and artistic and impossible not to like. I felt like I related to her exactly—minus the suicide part."[8]

In the film, Greta is shipped off to her grandparents' house for the summer. She falls in love with a cook at the restaurant where she works as a waitress. The plot centers around the pair's relationship. Greta's grandparents disapprove because of her boyfriend's criminal past.

They also worry because it is a mixed-race relationship. Academy Award winner Ellen Burstyn, Evan Ross, and Michael Murphy also appeared in the film.

In the drama *What Goes Up,* Duff played Lucy, a student in the 1980s mourning the death of her teacher who had committed suicide. A New York reporter, played by Steve Coogan, is sent to cover the Challenger space shuttle launch and becomes mixed up in the lives of some local students, including Lucy's. Duff had fun filming the movie in clothes and hairstyles from the 1980s. In the comedy *Stay Cool,* Duff played Shasta O'Neil, a high school senior. Shasta flirts with an author visiting her school and invites him to the prom. Duff costarred with Sean Astin, Chevy Chase, Mark Polish, and Josh Holloway.

Hilary Duff's fashion lines continue to thrive. She has sold more than 13 million records worldwide. And her acting career has never looked brighter. Duff always looks for fresh and exciting ways to keep her career moving forward. "I still haven't done all of the things I want to do," she said. "I still want to work hard."[9]

Her strong work ethic and positive attitude keep her on track in her personal life and in her professional life. "The older you get, you get a little tough and not so dreamy," she said. "But my spirit has stayed the same. It hasn't been tarnished by the business."[10]

Hilary Duff and her boyfriend Mike Comrie arrive at a screening of *Stay Cool* during the 2009 Tribeca Film Festival in New York City.

Hilary Duff would like to marry someday and have children, but not any time soon. She wants to focus on maintaining her balance and keeping her career moving forward. "As I get older, I want to challenge myself more and take more risks," she said, "but I don't like to plan too much ahead. I don't want to burn out. I always want to enjoy what I do."[11]

As an international celebrity, Hilary Duff flies from California to New York, zips up to Canada, then hops over to Europe or down to Australia. She juggles acting, singing, and running a fashion empire. A popular star, photographers snap her picture wherever she goes. Fans beg for her autograph. She has a busy schedule. But, regardless of what town she is in, Hilary Duff makes time to serve others.

Working with USA Harvest and Blessings in a Backpack, Duff continues her efforts to make sure every American has enough food to eat. She is also a spokesperson for Kids With a Cause and appears at fund-raising events for the group. The money they raise is used to supply "Comfort Zones" for pediatric patients. These play centers include DVD players, CD players, video game systems, arts and crafts activities, books, and toys. KWAC also buys blankets for children in homeless shelters and essentials for victims of natural disasters.

Duff also plans and organizes special programs and events for disadvantaged children. She takes them to theme parks, goes bowling with them, takes them horseback riding, or to the movies. "She is like this little angel that touches so many lives," said Linda Finnegan, founder of Kids With a Cause.[12]

Duff's involvement in Kids With a Cause made a strong impression on the many young people she served. Thousands of children wrote to Kids With a Cause and asked how they could help. Helping Hands was formed to allow every child the opportunity to help less fortunate children.

Helping Hands offers suggestions and examples for how ordinary children can lend a helping hand. "No matter how big or small of a contribution you make to help others, even a little, helps a lot," wrote Renee Rodrigues, special correspondent for the Helping Hands newsletter. "Sometimes the simplest ideas and littlest things can be the most fun and make a big difference to someone in need."[13]

Hilary Duff encourages her fans to believe in themselves and follow their dreams. "If you have a dream, go after it," she said, "keep on trying. It will pay off."[14] That philosophy has worked for Duff. She has loads of talent and is successful as an actress, singer, philanthropist, and businesswoman. She will remain a force in the entertainment industry for as long as she chooses to continue in that arena. But no matter what she does in the future, Hilary Duff will remember those less fortunate than herself. She will always be a celebrity with heart.

Chronology

1987— Hilary Erhard Duff is born on September 28 in Houston, Texas.

1993— Dances in the Columbus BalletMet holiday ballet *The Nutcracker*.

1996— Hilary, Haylie, and Susan Duff move to Los Angeles, California.

1997— Hilary earns a small role in the television miniseries *True Women*.

1998— Stars in the direct-to-video movie *Casper Meets Wendy*.

1999— Appears in the made-for-TV movie *The Soul Collector*; becomes a charter member of Kids With a Cause.

2000— Wins the Young Artist Award for Best Performance in a TV Movie or Pilot—Supporting Young Actress for *The Soul Collector*.

2001— Appears in the film *Human Nature*.

2001–2003 —Stars in the television series *Lizzie McGuire*.

2002— Stars in the Disney television movie *Cadet Kelly*; records the song "I Can't Wait" on the *Lizzie McGuire* CD; records "The Tiki, Tiki, Tiki Room" on the *Disneymania* CD; records the CD *Santa Claus Lane*; nominated for Favorite Television Actress at the Nickelodeon Kids' Choice Awards.

2003— Stars in the movie *Agent Cody Banks* with Frankie Muniz; stars in *The Lizzie McGuire Movie*; releases her first pop album, *Metamorphosis*, and number-one hit single, "So Yesterday"; appears in the film *Cheaper by the Dozen* with Steve Martin and Bonnie Hunt; becomes the official Youth Ambassador of Return to Freedom.

2004— Stars in the films *A Cinderella Story* and *Raise Your Voice*; launches fashion line Stuff by Hilary Duff; releases second album, *Hilary Duff*; performs in the United States and Canada on her *Most Wanted* music tour; wins Favorite Female Singer at Nickelodeon Kids' Choice Awards; wins the Today's Superstar Award at the Young Hollywood Awards; wins Best New Female Artist at the World Music Awards.

2005— Stars in the film *The Perfect Man* with Heather Locklear; appears in *Cheaper by the Dozen 2*; releases third CD, *Most Wanted*; performs in the United States and Australia on her *Still Most*

Wanted music tour; wins Favorite Movie Actress at Nickelodeon Kids' Choice Awards; begins collecting food with USA Harvest.

2006—Costars with her sister Haylie in *Material Girls*; performs in the United States, Mexico, Canada, and Europe on her *Still Most Wanted* music tour; serves on the Kids With a Cause International Council.

2007—Stuff by Hilary Duff is modeled at New York's Fashion Week; releases fourth CD, *Dignity*; performs in the United States and Canada on her *Dignity* music tour.

2008—Appears in *War, Inc.* with John Cusack; performs in Mexico, Brazil, and Australia on her *Dignity* music tour.

2009—Stars in the dramas *What Goes Up* and *Greta;* stars in the comedy *Stay Cool.*

2010—Movies *Provinces of Night, The Story of Bonnie and Clyde,* and *Foodfight!* to be released.

Filmography

*Note: Years correspond to scheduled release dates in the United States.

1997   *True Women*

1998   *Casper Meets Wendy*

1999   *The Soul Collector*

2001   *Human Nature*

2001–2003   *Lizzie McGuire*

2002   *Cadet Kelly*

2003   *Agent Cody Banks*

   The Lizzie McGuire Movie

   Cheaper by the Dozen

2004   *A Cinderella Story*

   Raise Your Voice

2005   *The Perfect Man*

   Cheaper by the Dozen 2

2006   *Material Girls*

2008   *War, Inc.*

2009   *Greta*

   What Goes Up

   Stay Cool

2010   *Foodfight!*

   Provinces of Night

   The Story of Bonnie and Clyde

Discography

2002   *Santa Claus Lane*

2003   *Metamorphosis*

2004   *Hilary Duff*

2005   *Most Wanted* (compilation)

2007   *Dignity*

2008   *Best of Hilary Duff*

Chapter Notes

Chapter 1
Giving Back

1. "Hilary Duff's Blog: Blessings In a Backpack," *Hilary Duff*, June 20, 2007, <http://www.hilaryduff.com/portal/members/blog.asp?> (January 23, 2008).
2. Tara Hettinger, "Celebrating Blessings," *NewsAndTribune.com*, October 24, 2008, <http://www.newsandtribune.com/homepage/local_story_298121820.html?keyword=leadpicturestory> (December 19, 2008).
3. Tara Hettinger, "Q & A: One-on-One With Hilary Duff," *NewsAndTribune.com*, October 24, 2008, <http://www.newsandtribune.com/clarkcounty/local_story_298123237.html> (December 19, 2008).
4. "Hilary Duff's Blog: Blessings In a Backpack."
5. Hettinger, "Q & A: One-on-One With Hilary Duff."
6. Valerie Boey, "Hilary Duff Visits Orlando School," *My Fox Orlando*, May 23, 2008, <http://www.myfoxorlando.com/dpp/about_us/Hilary_Duff_visits_Orlando_School> (December 19, 2008).
7. Hettinger, "Celebrating Blessings."
8. "Hilary Duff's Blog: Thank You!!!" *Hilary Duff*, September 20, 2007, <http://www.hilaryduff.com/portal/members/blog.asp?> (January 23, 2008).
9. "Empowering YOUth: Home," *Kids With a Cause*, 2008, <http://www.kidswithacause.org/home.shtml> (February 4, 2008).
10. William C. Reynolds, "Hilary Duff: A Texas Metamorphosis," *Cowboys and Indians*, June 2004, p. 103.
11. "Hilary Duff's Blog: Much Love," *Hilary Duff*, July 25, 2007, <http://www.hilaryduff.com/portal/members/blog.asp?> (January 23, 2008).

12. "Happy 21st Birthday Hilary," *Hilary Duff*, September 27, 2008, <http://www.hilaryduff.com/portal/news/news.asp?item=5000506> (October 2, 2008).

13. Ibid.

Chapter 2
The Early Years

1. Karen S. Schneider, "Tween Queen," *People*, May 19, 2003, p. 84.
2. Jill Rappaport and Wendy Wilkinson, *People We Know, Horses They Love* (Emmaus, Pa.: Rodale, Inc., 2004), p. 147.
3. Ibid., p. 146.
4. William C. Reynolds, "Hilary Duff: A Texas Metamorphosis," *Cowboys and Indians*, June 2004, p. 100.
5. "Meet My Parents," *Popstar! Collector's Edition–Hilary Duff: Inside Her World!* October 2003, p. 20.
6. Ibid.
7. Taylor Hanson, "Hilary Duff," *Interview*, February 2004, p. 123.
8. Janelle Brown, "Hilary Duff," *Seventeen*, August 2004, p. 158.
9. "Meet My Parents," p. 20.
10. Ibid.
11. "On a Different Note: Tired of Being Lizzie McGuire," *Sunday Herald*, April 23, 2006, <http://findarticles.com/> (June 5, 2009).
12. Tim Carvell, "The Girl In the Bubble," *Entertainment Weekly*, May 9, 2003, p. 36.
13. "Teen Player," *People*, January 28, 2002, p. 71.
14. Brown, p. 158.
15. Kate Stroup, "Girl Power," *Newsweek*, March 17, 2003, p. 57.
16. Fred Shuster, "The Girl Next Door, Hilary Duff Is More Than a Match for her Lovable TV Persona," *Los Angeles Daily News*, February 7, 2002, <http://www.thefreelibrary.com/> (June 5, 2009).

Chapter 3
Suddenly a Star

1. Kimberly Speight, "Ones To Watch," *Hollywood Reporter*, November 20–26, 2001, p. S-20.
2. Hannah Storm, "Hilary Duff's Star Rising," *CBS Early Show*, May 7, 2003.
3. Fred Shuster, "The Girl Next Door," *Los Angeles Daily News*, February 7, 2002, <http://www.thefreelibrary.com/> (June 5, 2009).

4. Hilary Duff, "Who's News," *Time For Kids*, May 2, 2003, p. 8.
5. Clifford Pugh, "Perks and Chores: Hilary Duff Stays On the Run," *Houston Chronicle*, April 11, 2002.
6. Laura Fries, "Lizzie McGuire," *Variety*, January 15, 2001, p. 60.
7. "Hilary Duff Chat Transcript," *Walt Disney Records*, December 20, 2002, <http://disney.go.com/disneyrecords/Song-Albums/santaclauslane/chat.html> (March 11, 2008).
8. Alicia Clott, "What's Hilary Thinking?" *Girls' Life*, April/May 2002, p. 45.
9. Speight, p. S-20.
10. "Agent Cody Banks (2003)," *Internet Movie Database*, <http://www.imdb.com/title/tt0313911/> (September 26, 2008).
11. Storm.
12. Laura C. Girardi, "Hilary Duff, Actress," *Time For Kids*, April 28, 2003, <http://www.timeforkids.com/TFK/kids/news/story/0,28277,447628,00.html> (April 18, 2008).
13. Cathy Frisinger, "Sweet Life As Lizzie," *Toronto Star*, March 27, 2003.
14. Steve Traiman, "Hilary Duff," *Billboard*, July 5, 2003, p. 33.

Chapter 4

Making Music

1. Craig Rosen, "Hilary Duff: A Performer's Metamorphosis," *Billboard,* January 31, 2004, p. 14.
2. Ibid.
3. Ibid.
4. William C. Reynolds, "Hilary Duff: A Texas Metamorphosis," *Cowboys and Indians*, June 2004, p. 99.
5. Bonnie Laufer-Krebs, "The Stuff On Hilary Duff," *Teen Tribute,* Fall 2003, p. 26.
6. Rosen, p. 14.
7. Richard Corliss, "The Fresh-Face Factory," *Time*, April 14, 2003, <http://www.time.com/time/magazine/article/0,9171,1004641,00.html> (June 8, 2009).
8. Ben Rayner, "Duff's Double Life," *Toronto Star*, April 25, 2007.
9. Kate O'Hare, "Hilary Duff Is All Sweet 16 For the WB," *Zap2It.com*, September 25, 2003, <http://www.ebscohost.com/> (June 9, 2009).

10. *Hilary Duff: The Girl Can Rock*, DVD (Burbank, Calif.: Buena Vista Home Entertainment, Inc., 2004).

11. Katy Vine, "Teeny Popper," *Texas Monthly*, April 2004, p. 82.

12. Ibid., p. 80.

13. *Hilary Duff: The Girl Can Rock.*

14. Susanne Ault, "Duff Proves She's Not 'So Yesterday' On Tour," *Billboard*, December 13, 2003, p. 30.

15. Jodi Bryson, "Life After Lizzie," *Girls' Life*, August/September 2003, p. 46.

16. Susan Wloszczyna, "For Duff's Next Role, the More the Merrier," *USA Today*, May 23, 2003.

17. Marine Bury, "On The Set With Hilary Duff," *YM*, October 2003, <http://www.ym.com/stars/inthespotlight/sep0203.jsp> (March 13, 2008).

18. Jenn Spence, "Duff Was Late But Still Great," *Toronto Star*, March 25, 2004.

19. "Hilary Duff: Chat Transcript," *MuchMusic.com*, September 8, 2003, <http://www.muchmusic.com/tv/transcripts/index.asp?artist=790&tranID=316> (April 23, 2008).

20. "Hilary Duff: The Ultimate Superstar!" *Popstar!* April 2005, p. 23.

Chapter 5

Duff's Stuff

1. Jennifer A. Kingson, "Teen Pop Star's Latest Project: A Gift Card," *American Banker*, October 17, 2003, p. 7.

2. Dana Flavelle, "Zellers Unveils Hilary Duff Clothing Line," *Toronto Star*, March 13, 2004.

3. Rosie Amodio, "Hangin' Out With Hilary," *Teen People*, November 2004, p. 95.

4. Lori Berger, "Hilary Duff," *CosmoGirl*, March 2004, p. 128.

5. Margo Varadi, "The Stuff Of Tween Dreams," *Toronto Star*, March 13, 2004.

6. *Hilary Duff: The Girl Can Rock*, DVD (Burbank, Calif.: Buena Vista Home Entertainment, Inc., 2004).

7. Marie Morreale, "Behind the Scenes With Hilary Duff," *Scholastic Scope*, December 8, 2003, p. 13.

8. "Just 4 Kids," *Return to Freedom*, 2003, <http://www.returntofreedom.org/kids/kids.html> (February 4, 2008).

9. William C. Reynolds, "Hilary Duff: A Texas Metamorphosis," *Cowboys and Indians,* June 2004, p. 96.
10. "A Cinderella Story," *Popstar! Collector's Edition—Hilary Duff: Inside Her World!* October 2003, p. 69.
11. Carla Hay, "Hilary Duff: Living a 'Cinderella' Dream," *Billboard,* July 31, 2004, p. 12.
12. Roger Ebert, "Do Yourself a Favor, Skip 'Cinderella Story,'" *Chicago Sun-Times,* July 16, 2004.
13. Stephen Hunter, "Skip This Ball: 'Cinderella' Is a Limp Take on the Tale," *Washington Post,* July 16, 2004.
14. Nick Duerden, "The Golden Girl," *Blender,* October 2004, <http://www.blender.com/guide/67648/golden-girl.html> (March 13, 2008).
15. "Hilary Duff," *Scholastic Action,* January 3, 2005, p. 5.
16. Amodio, p. 95.
17. *Hilary Duff: The Girl Can Rock.*
18. Duerden.
19. Kate Stroup, "Girl Power," *Newsweek,* March 17, 2003, p. 57.
20. Amodio, p. 94.
21. "Music From The Heart!" *Popstar!* April 2005, p. 8.
22. Duerden.

Chapter 6

Doing It All

1. Doug Sample, "Duff Helps Kick Off National Military Families Week," *American Forces Press Service,* June 11, 2005, <http://www.defenselink.mil/news/newsarticle.aspx?id=16432> (June 8, 2009).
2. Jeff Johnson, "Of Course She Loves The Smiths," *Jane,* September 2005, p. 140.
3. Vincent J. Schodolski, "Hilary Duff Is, Like, In a Good Place Right Now," *Hilaryontheweb.com,* June 2005, <http://www.hilaryontheweb.com/interviews/interviews/Hilary_Duff_is_like_in_a_good_place_right_now.html> (August 13, 2008).
4. Claudia Puig, "'The Perfect Man' Doesn't Measure Up," *USA Today,* June 17, 2005, <http://www.usatoday.com/life/movies/reviews/2005-06-16-the-perfect-man_x.htm?loc=interstitialskip> (June 8, 2009).

5. Stephen Hunter, "Hilary Duff's Ill-Conceived 'Perfect Man,'" *Washington Post,* June 17, 2005.

6. Lola Ogunnaike, "Just Wants to Have (Clean) Fun," *New York Times,* October 13, 2004, <http://www.nytimes.com/2004/10/13/arts/music/13duff.html> (June 8, 2009).

7. Michelle Tauber, "Sweet 18," *People,* June 27, 2005, p. 131.

8. Sherri Wood, "We're In the Duff," *Sun Media,* August 14, 2005.

9. Johnson, p. 138.

10. "Hilary Duff to Donate $250,000 to Victims of Hurricane Katrina," *Business Wire,* September 1, 2005, <http://findarticles.com/> (July 30, 2008).

11. Tauber, pp. 130–131.

12. Abbey Goodman, "Hilary Duff: The Nicest Brat," *MTV,* November 12, 2004, <http://www.mtv.com/bands/d/duff_hilary/news_feature/041115/index.jhtml> (May 28, 2008).

13. "Hilary Duff's Changing Diet," *People,* August 17, 2005, <http://www.people.com/people/article/0,26334,1094660,00.html> (July 3, 2008).

14. "Transformations: Hilary Duff," *People,* May 9, 2005, p. 96.

15. Dennis Pollock, "Campaign Hopes California's Children 'Stay Fit' and 'Eat Right,'" *The Fresno Bee,* September 24, 2005, redOrbit.com, 2009, <http://www.redorbit.com/news/health/254469/campaign_hopes_californias_children_stay_fit_and_eat_right/index.html> (June 8, 2009).

Chapter 7

A Year of Changes

1. James Reaney, "Duff Inspires Magic Moment From Young Fans," *CANOE—Jam! Music,* January 21, 2006, <http://jam.canoe.ca/Music/Artists/D/Duff_Hilary/ConcertReviews/2006/01/22/1406148.html> (June 8, 2009).

2. Carrie Borzillo-Vrenna, "Teen People's 25 Hottest: Hilary Duff," *Teen People,* June 2006, p. 54.

3. Melanie Abrahams, "End Hunger Now," *Seventeen,* May 2007, p. 108.

4. Shawna Malcom, "Hilary Duff: Hollywood's Most Wanted," *Cosmopolitan,* March 2006, p. 40.

5. Denise Henry, "Hilary Duff," *Scholastic Action,* September 5, 2005, p. 5.

6. Jodi Bryson, "The Very Fortunate Hilary Duff," *Girls' Life,* August/September 2005, p. 87.

7. "Hilary Duff's First Fragrance," *People,* September 4, 2006, p. 150.

8. Alice Smellie, "Celebrity Scents On Trial," *Daily Mail,* March 12, 2007, p. 52.

9. "Hilary Duff To Appear In EA's the Sims 2 Pets," *PC Games,* October 17, 2006, <http://www.gamespot.com/pc/strategy/thesims2pets/news.html?sid=6159354> (April 22, 2008).

10. Elysa Gardner, "The Focus Is On Hilary," *USA Today,* April 3, 2007, <http://www.usatoday.com/life/music/news/2007-04-02-hilary-duff-inisde_N.htm> (June 8, 2009).

11. Abbey Goodman, "Hilary Duff: The Nicest Brat," *MTV,* November 12, 2004, <http://www.mtv.com/bands/d/duff_hilary/news_feature/041115/index.jhtml> (May 28, 2008).

Chapter 8

Dignity

1. "Hilary Duff," *People,* February 26, 2007, p. 149.

2. Kwala Mandel, "Sexy and the Single Girl Starring Hilary Duff," *InStyle,* Summer 2007, vol. 1, no. 2, p. 44, <http://www.proquest.com/en-US/> (June 9, 2009).

3. Barry Shlachter, "Business Insider Column: Shlachter, Perotin, Fuquay and Co.," *Fort Worth Star-Telegram,* August 9, 2007.

4. "Hilary Duff's Blog: Wow! What a Week," *Hilary Duff,* March 21, 2007, <http://www.hilaryduff.com/portal/members/blog.asp?> (January 23, 2008).

5. *Hilary Duff: Dignity,* DVD (Burbank, Calif.: Hollywood Records, Inc., 2007).

6. Ben Rayner, "Duff's Double Life," *Toronto Star,* April 25, 2007.

7. Allison Prato, "The Last Temptation of Hilary Duff," *Maxim,* August 2007, p. 86.

8. Jonathan Bernstein, "Duff In a Huff," *Entertainment Weekly,* April 6, 2007, p. 75.

9. "Hilary Duff's Blog: Dignity Release Party," *Hilary Duff,* April 4, 2007, <http://www.hilaryduff.com/portal/members/blog.asp?> (January 23, 2008).

10. "Hilary Duff's Blog: More Big News!" *Hilary Duff,* May 2, 2007, <http://www.hilaryduff.com/portal/members/blog.asp?> (January 23, 2008).

Chapter Notes

Chapter 9
A Bright Future

1. Molly Fahner, "Hilary Duff Gets Daring," *Cosmopolitan,* January 2008, p. 30.
2. Chris Harris, "Hilary Duff On Controversial Miley Cyrus Pics: 'Who Am I To Judge?'" *MTV,* April 29, 2008, <http://www.mtv.com/news/articles/1586479/20080429/duff_hilary.jhtml> (May 31, 2008).
3. Allison Prato, "The Last Temptation of Hilary Duff," *Maxim,* August 2007, p. 86.
4. Linda Solomon, *The Key: Celebrated People Unlock Their Secrets To Life* (New York: Stewart, Tabori and Chang, 2007), p. 22.
5. Joe Leydon, "Hilary Duff Breaks Out of Her Shell," *Houston Chronicle,* July 11, 2008, <http://www.chron.com/CDA/archives/archive.mpl?id=2008_4596637> (June 8, 2009).
6. Shawn Adler, "John Cusack Calls Hilary Duff 'A Revelation'; Has His Eye On 'Watchmen,'" *MTV,* June 13, 2007, <http://www.mtv.com/movies/news/articles/1562299/20070612/story.jhtml> (May 31, 2008).
7. Lewis Beale, "Hilary Duff Chats About Sexy Role In 'War, Inc.,'" *Newsday,* May 22, 2008, <http://www.newsday.com/services/newspaper/printedition/sunday/fanfare/ny-fffast5685773may18,0,6146500.story> (June 8, 2009).
8. Merle Ginsberg, "The One To Watch: Hilary Duff," *Maxim,* January 2009, p. 50.
9. "Hilary Duff," *People,* February 26, 2007, p. 149.
10. Brooke Hauser, "Good to The Bone," *Allure,* May 2008, p. 258.
11. Iain Blair, "Hilary Duff," *Daily Variety,* October 5, 2007, p. 23.
12. Personal interview with Linda Finnegan, founder of Kids With a Cause, September 23, 2008.
13. Renee Rodrigues, "Empowering YOUth: Helping Hands," *Kids With a Cause,* 2008, <http://www.kidswithacause.org/club.shtml> (September 24, 2008).
14. "Hilary Duff Chat Transcript," *Walt Disney Records,* December 20, 2002, <http://disney.go.com/disneyrecords/Song-Albums/santaclauslane/chat.html> (March 11, 2008).

Further Reading

Boone, Mary. *Hilary Duff: Total Hilary, Metamorphosis, Lizzie McGuire and More!* Chicago: Triumph Entertainment, 2003.

Dougherty, Terri. *Hilary Duff.* Farmington Hills, Mich.: Lucent Books, 2008.

Krulik, Nancy. *Hilary Duff: A Not-So-Typical Teen.* New York: Simon Spotlight, 2003.

Rettenmund, Matthew. *Hilary Duff: All Access.* New York: Berkley Boulevard Books, 2005.

Whiting, Jim. *Hilary Duff.* Broomall, Pa.: Moon Crest Publishers, Inc., 2008.

Internet Addresses

Hilary Duff
http://www.hilaryduff.com

Kids With a Cause
http://www.kidswithacause.org

Return to Freedom
http://www.returntofreedom.org

USA Harvest
http://www.usaharvest.com

Index

Index